William Russell Dunham

The science of vital force.

Its plan, division of function, and operative methods in health and disease

William Russell Dunham

The science of vital force.
Its plan, division of function, and operative methods in health and disease

ISBN/EAN: 9783337775407

Printed in Europe, USA, Canada, Australia, Japan

Cover: Foto ©ninafisch / pixelio.de

More available books at **www.hansebooks.com**

THE

SCIENCE OF VITAL

ITS PLAN, DIVISION OF FU
AND OPERATIVE METHOD
HEALTH AND DISEASE

AN INVOLUNTARY AGENCY OF NA
. CAN BE HARNESSED AND UT

—

BY

W. R. DUNHAM, M.

AUTHOR OF "HIGHER MEDICAL CU

BOSTON:

DAMRELL AND UPHAM,

The Old Corner Bookstore.

1894.

University Press:
JOHN WILSON AND SON, CAMBRIDGE, U.S.A.

CONTENTS.

PAGE

INTRODUCTION 7

CHAPTER

I. STATEMENT OF THE SITUATION . . . 9

II. THE PLAN OF OPERATIVE VITAL
FORCE. DIVISION OF DUTIES AND
ULTIMATE FUNCTIONS 21

III. APPLICATION OF VITAL PRINCIPLES
AND SIGNIFICANT PARAGRAPHS . . 34

IV. ULTIMATE VITAL PROPERTIES . . . 50

V. FUNDAMENTAL PRINCIPLES IN RELA-
TIONS WITH DISEASE 77

VI. DISEASE GERMS 108

VII. TOLERATION 124

VIII. MEDICAL PRACTICE 131

IX. SENSATION AND SENSIBILITY 151

X. PNEUMONIA 167

XI. MISCELLANEOUS PARAGRAPHS . . . 180

INTRODUCTION.

THE object of this volume is to designate and demonstrate the fundamental principles of THE SCIENCE OF VITAL FORCE,— a department of natural science that is directly applicable to the preservation of health and the treatment of disease. It is implied in fundamental principles and laws of Nature not yet recognized and presented for consideration, and is a department of science that will require a large amount of literature to illustrate its practical application to individual and national affairs. It also implies a revolution of the recognized plan and principles of a department that has been erroneously presented,— a revolution as significant as was effected in the ideal change of the centre of the solar system, and the principles involved being as capable of a positive demonstration. We allege that medical practice, both regular and irregular, is based on imaginary fundamental principles as unreal as was the Ptolemaic system of astronomy, on theories that are insufficient for the safe guidance of treatment, and dangerous in their application.

STONEHAM, MASS.

THE SCIENCE OF VITAL FORCE.

I.

STATEMENT OF THE SITUATION.

Every now and then a man's mind is stretched by a new idea, and never shrinks back to its former dimensions.—O. W. HOLMES.

WE shall call attention to a department of natural science not taught in the schools and institutions of learning, — a science implied in that agency called "vital force," a subject referred to in medical literature as being too profound for this age, and which is thus relegated to future generations for a solution. It is a department awaiting the recognition of living outgrowths of actual principles in Nature.

This science is not capable of being verified from accepted fundamental principles now recognized, but can be demonstrated in the functions of the living human organism. The nature and laws of the force of gravitation have been solved, and are now being taught as operative in astronomical science, while that agency called "vital force" is receiving little or no consideration from any department of literature. We shall present many nice distinctions for adjustment; and the differentiation of the operative significance of the agencies called "mind," "life," and "vital force," may not appear distinct at first, but will be defined later. We shall, however, deal mostly with the operative methods and functions of that agency called "vital force," as applied to the human organism in the matter of health and disease.

It is difficult at first to recognize that in the department of living nature a serious mistake has been made relative to the fundamental operative principles, that a different plan, wholly unlike what is now taught, explains better, and correctly, the situation.

In illustration of the premises to be considered, no better comparison can be made than by reference to the condition of the science of astronomy in the time of Ptolemy. At that time all were familiar with astronomical phenomena, but the mind had failed to grasp the plan making it possible to explain how such phenomena were produced. Thus they were trying to explain appearances from an imaginary basis. Medical theories are now projected from similar premises. That is, a great variety of the phenomena presented by the living human organism are alleged to be produced by an *active principle*, not vital, — an agency wholly imaginary. The *vital force agency*, as implied in the ultimate functions of operative life-processes, is a subject confessed in medical literature to be outside the realm of comprehension. Therefore, the recognition of the *science* of vital force must be implied in the development of new ideas of Nature's methods.

We are informed in history that the ancient scholar Pliny, who lived previous to the third century A. D., gave credit to Acron as being the first to apply philosophical reason, in explanation of medicinal relations, to the human organism. And to him this generation is indebted for that unfortunate interpretation, which has been perpetuated to our day, in the recognition of an "active medical principle." We allege, and shall demonstrate, that the doctrine of "active medical property" is a misnomer in phraseology, and an ideal delusion of serious and great magnitude in its application.

What is now alleged to be an "active medical principle" was formerly called a "medical power" — an ideal and imaginary agency, which is said to be in association with material medicine, that may operate and act on the organs of the living human system. We are also required to give credit to the same authority for the originality of the recognition of a different and undefined agency, which was presumed to find its way into the human system, and to operate disastrously to the well being of the individual; which disturbance was called " disease."

If Acron was correct in his interpretations, there is illustrated a singular incident, worthy of eulogistic commemoration for all time, implied in that keen perception of intellect which was capable of grasping the nature and plan of such relations, which have ever remained satisfactory with all later generations; while that less mysteriously profound problem of determining the centre of the solar system awaited the advent of Copernicus more than twelve centuries later.

This imaginary agency — " active medical principle " — has been equally as acceptable and satisfactory to cultured civilization for centuries as was the ancient ideal centre of the solar system. Thus there has seemed to be no occasion for overhauling the alleged plans and methods of Nature that are implied in such relations, which practically inflict immeasurable and serious inconvenience upon cultured and civilized nations.

Acron recognized an " active cause of disease," possessed of a riotous disposition, and also an alleged " medical power," now called " active medical property," which was presumed to put to rout the former invader, restore order, and exercise curative influence.

The reader of modern medical literature of the present day will discover but slight modification of fundamental premises, unlike those presented for consideration by the ancient mind. The ideal " active cause of disease " is still recognized as a disturbing agent, associated with some kind of material and alleged " disease germs." The principle of activity, formerly called " a medical power," is now changed to an " active medical property ; " at the same time, however, the phrase " medical power " is of common use in medical literature. *Vital force* is recognized as that agency which executes the constructive organic function and structural repairs; and also as exercising in disease an influence called the "efforts of nature." And what the vital force is not alleged to do, in the name of "efforts of nature," is presumed to be done by that *reserve force* of alleged practical utility called the "active medical property," which is accepted as capable of temporarily operating the functional machinery of human life until the vital force rallies to the rescue.

If medical literature means anything, such is the true representation of the existing situation in the department of alleged medical science.

Notwithstanding that such ideas are supported by the doctrines of current medical literature, we shall try to illustrate the fact, through the Science of Vital Force, that the *cause* of disease is *passive*, and also that the doctrine of an "active medical property" is a delusion. The *active* properties are all *vital*, although an eminent medical writer of this generation thus states: "This generation and generations to come will have passed to their everlasting rest before a discovery of the secret of vital activity is made." This discovery is already made, to be illustrated in the Science of Vital Force; and when understood, which is not a difficult matter, cultured civilization will recognize that the fundamental doctrines of alleged medical science are as crude and inapplicable as the ancient astronomical doctrine advanced by Ptolemy.

This whole matter is easy of comprehension when considered from a correct standpoint. No one could comprehend the Copernican system of astronomy with Ptolemaic ideas. No one can understand the nature of vital force while seeking to explain the manifestation of living phenomena as being produced by some agency, not vital, that was acting on the human organism.

In our efforts to present intelligently the nature, laws, and operative methods of vital force, we are required to begin with a recognition unlike that which prevails with the agency called "the force of gravitation," in which department it is not possible to recognize more than one method, one ultimate function; while the science of vital force is implied in a compound *primary* function, and in four different, equally *ultimate* methods of vital action, — a fact apparently not recognized by medical writers and scientists.

In calling attention to this department of Nature, we doubtless may be laboring under disadvantages similar to those which existed when it was sought to make acceptable the idea of a different centre of the solar system. The already accepted centre was so satisfactory that it required more skill to eliminate the false doctrine than to explain the harmony, utility, and advantage of the natural plan implied in a different centre. The theory and doctrine of "active medical properties" has been accepted for more than fifteen centuries without a recognized protest considered worthy of review; and like seeing the sun revolve around the earth, both cultured and uncultured minds have seen what this "active medical property" was doing, provided we accept this testimony. We confess that it will be difficult in this age of intelligence to eliminate long cherished ideas, and to accept the situation we allege, without the presentation of a volume of incontrovertible testimony from Nature.

At first we are confronted with this rational inference, that it does not seem credible that the analytical mind, particularly of the last half century, could have been mistaken in the nature of this problem. The same, however, was doubtless said of the ideal earth-centre of the solar system, after thirteen hundred years of acceptance, when Copernicus recorded his protest. This science is not obscured by its profundity, but it has simply been over-looked, existing in a place where the human mind has never had occasion to make research. It has remained among the hidden mysteries of Nature, largely

because there has been accepted an ideal
substitute for vital force,—an agency not
vital, called the "active medical principle."

Every department of natural science executed by the forces of Nature is presented
in accordance with a pre-arranged plan; and
unless we recognize the correct plan, it is
impossible to comprehend the operative proceedings of that special department. To
make plain the distinction between the
accepted plan as now taught, and the plan
that we are to suggest for the study of this
department of Nature implied in the Science
of Vital Force, we would say that the present
accepted, erroneous, and ideal plan is implied in three unlike divisions of alleged
active *principles*,—the active vital principle,
the principle implied in the "active cause
of disease," and the "active medical property;" whereas the plan that we shall allege and demonstrate is implied in one
kind of active principle,—the *active vital*

principle, having four distinct ultimate vital properties.

The difference of plan as an intellectual question implies an operative distinction equal to the difference between the two alleged centres of the solar system.

II.

THE PLAN OF OPERATIVE VITAL FORCE. DIVISION OF DUTIES AND ULTIMATE FUNCTIONS.

VITAL power is that active principle which constructs and preserves the human organism, executing its mission in the universe with as much precision and conformity to law and method as prevails in the departments of inorganic science. The inorganic force called "gravitation" executes those changeable phenomena presented in astronomical science, while the vital force executes those phenomena of natural science implied in conditions of health and disease, and operative proceedings which succeed from medicinal relations.

The study of the human system as now taught in the schools has its beginning with physiological functions and anatomical structures; while with the plan implied in the Science of Vital Force it is required that we begin further back, — that we make research, and determine what divisions there may be of ultimate vital functions that enable such physiological functions and anatomical structures to be thus executed and arranged. In other words, we must determine what constitute the essential and primary divisions of life functions, that as a whole make possible the execution of such proceedings. To say that such are organic human life functions, undefined, is not sufficient. It is necessary to grasp in idea certain great and underlying primal principles of organic human life, that have beginning and existence even before physiological and anatomical functions can be made operative.

We are about to start on an important journey of ideal research, — a research that may reward us with a correct recognition of the nature of vital force. Therefore it is necessary to determine something that vital

force does, that we can call by a name, —
some isolated ultimate function that can be
defined and demonstrated beyond all controversy.   And whatever such function (or functions) may be, it will be that something
which is done, which constitutes its nature.
We are at the most critical stage of this ideal
beginning; and we must begin right, and
make sure that none who come after us
can recognize a function and method of this
agency which we fail to discover; also that
what we define will be so susceptible of
demonstration that no contradiction can be
supported.   We cannot recognize its nature
in a single ultimate function that can be
expressed as a unit; but we are required to
interpret its nature as existing in four units,
four beginnings, four different functions, —
each unlike the other, and no part of the
other; each an ultimate function that can be
defined, verified, and demonstrated in unmis-
takable phenomena presented by the living
human organism, constituting in its four

divisions and unlike functions of vital properties the complete total and aggregate of vital methods, from which basis all the subsequent operations of life, in health and disease, are dependent. And we make use of the following names and terms as being representative of such four ultimate vital properties: SENSIBILITY, INSTINCT, SENSATION, and CONTRACTILITY.

We shall but briefly outline the function and distinction of each vital property in this place, but later will take up each division with a more extended illustration.

Sensibility. This term is used to represent certain life abilities comprised in all the variety of brain functions and conscious intelligence. This vital property is implied in the ability to command and execute voluntary acts, having perceptive abilities that may recognize things, conditions, and relations both in contact with the organism and external and beyond contact; that is, at all distances. It is the mind property, — that property of life which superintends all the voluntary acts.

Instinct. This is a vital property wholly unlike sensibility. It presides over the involuntary acts, superintending the construction of the organic body. Sensibility voluntarily supplies the material for constructive purpose, while instinct superintends the use and application of such material in the process of organic growth. The instinct superintends not only the disposition to be made of nutritive material, but the method of eliminating all foreign material that has been introduced into the human organism by accident or design. Instinct, as an ultimate vital property, has no other function except to superintend conditions, and to dispose of material having contact relations with the living organism. Sensibility is the commander-in-chief of the voluntary acts, while instinct is commander-in-chief of all involuntary acts manifested by the living organism. Instinct is a vital property pervading all the

living tissues, while sensibility is a vital
property not pervading all the tissues.

Sensation.　This is a vital property whose
function is wholly unlike those already mentioned.　It is a vital property expressed by
certain nerves, whose function is implied in
conveying information of existing conditions
and the presence of material contacts both
to sensibility and to instinct.　That is, com-
paratively speaking, sensation is a kind of
telegraph that makes known to the other vital
properties, or enables such other vital properties to hold practical relations with, existing
conditions and material contact relations, —
relations that may require attention from one
or both of those vital properties before
mentioned.

The means through which this vital property communicates such facts are implied in
an experience of varied sensations called
"feelings," which are produced by contacts,
and which are implied in all kinds of sensations, from exquisite sensational pleasures to

excruciating pain. The language of this vital property is the language of experienced sensation implied in all kinds of sensational feeling. It has no other function, it can execute no other duty. It was created for no other purpose than to experience feeling from con-· tact. And the silent language which it speaks thus communicates with sensibility and instinct, each being made aware of duties requiring the attention of both. The term "irritability" may represent either a disagreeable sensibility or a disagreeable sensation, but does not imply a different vital property. Some sensations are known and relate only to the consciousness, requiring attention solely from the function of sensibibity. Other sensations have practical relations only with the function of instinct, and are unknown by the sensibility as having existence.

In this distinction of the relations of sensation are implied important facts to be recognized later in association with the causes of disease. Sensibility executes its function at all distances, while sensation executes function only at insensible distances developed by causes existing in immediate contact. In medical literature the terms " sensibility " and " sensation " are used as synonyms in their application to the affairs of the human organism, obscuring all idea of difference between the functions of the two unlike vital properties, — the term "sensation" being frequently used for a brain function, while the term " sensibility " is made applicable to the representation of existing feelings of the lower extremities ; thus making it as impossible to solve and comprehend many of the problems of human life affairs as it would be to solve mathematical problems without distinction of idea between the application of division and multiplication.

Contractility. This is a vital property manifested by the contraction and alternate relaxation of muscular fibre.

This property may be considered as an invisible instrument of motion in the hands of both the instinct and sensibility. Sensation may have relation to certain facts that require the attention of instinct applied to the function of involuntary action. At other times, the sensation may relate to the sensibility in such way as to require that some duty shall be executed by a voluntary act. Thus contractility is a vital property to be made operative by both the instinct and the sensibility. In other words, sensibility presides over voluntary contractility, while instinct presides over involuntary contractility. Contractility is the animal strength property. Abstract thought implies the direct exercise of the vital property of sensibility. The mind does not effect voluntary muscular motion directly, but employs the vital property of contractility to execute this function. The same exercise of contractility can be made operative, and thus used by instinct to exercise muscular motion even after decapitation, by applying the galvanic current to cause irritable sensation.

We trust the reader will recognize the distinction implied between the direct and the indirect operation of a vital property. The science of vital force is implied in a great multiplicity of such distinctions.

We have thus outlined briefly the function of each of the ultimate vital properties and the unlike duties they perform, which in the aggregate are operative in producing all the visible phenomena presented by the living human organism. We trust the reader will be able to determine that one vital property is not the other, and that the problems of organic human life have their solution predicated on the nature and executive functions of the co-operative vital properties.

It is apparent that each of the ultimate vital properties executes unlike functions, while it requires the exercise of all those vital properties to execute physiological function and to construct anatomical product. Thus we trust that the premises are made clear;

that we begin with a study of life functions, which antedate physiological functions.

Reader, have you any exceptions to file relative to the number of ultimate vital properties, more or less; and whether or not such functions as mentioned are entitled to be considered as ultimate vital properties? Can you recognize in the human organism any vital function not entitled to be included in the four properties described? Do you think Nature does, or does not, supply and present the existence of ultimate functions that can be verified, in order to demonstrate the correctness of the working plan as here presented?

To understand the nature of disease, — not its *appearance*, but how it is produced, — and how to prevent and how to cure, and how to take advantage of fleeting opportunities; and also to understand the relation of *materia medica* to the human system, in addition to the knowledge of its relational *effects*, it is essential to become familiar with the operative and co-operative functions of the four vital properties in all the affairs of human life. And while it was necessary to eliminate the ideal earth-centre of the solar system to enable the science of astronomy to be developed, it will be equally important and imperative to eliminate the doctrine of ideal " active medical property," — that ideal and imaginary agency which is presumed to act and exercise an influence with the involuntary department of human life affairs.

This doctrine and idea of " active medical property " has been kept alive and perpetuated by a conventional acceptance based on appearances, which is wholly in violation of the nature of things, and as unreal of correct representation as the alleged earth-centre, and having no more scientific meaning than a telegraphic cypher code.

It is a singular fact that in the study of this subject we are confronted with a very peculiar paradox. Notwithstanding this doctrine of " active medical property " constitutes a serious obstacle in the pathway of a recognized science of vital force, it is not possible to eliminate such delusion until a comprehension and recognized demonstration can be developed of the nature and functions of the ultimate properties of vital force, and of their co-operative methods of procedure in the affairs of health and disease. A knowledge of the special function of each of the ultimate vital properties, and of their co-operative relations, contributes to a comprehension of the nature of every variety of disease, its proper treatment and the *modus operandi* of medicine. Such knowledge contributes an advantage equal to that which the knowledge of the first four principles of arithmetic contributes to the solution of problems in higher mathematics, and is no less indispensable.

III.

APPLICATION OF VITAL PRINCIPLES AND SIGNIFICANT PARAGRAPHS.

WE shall call attention to the application of separate vital properties in execution of physiological functions, only sufficient to make illustration of simple problems that may lead to the elucidation of the more complex.

The vital property, sensibility, makes use of the voluntary, contractility, to introduce within the stomach the nutritive material necessary for organic constructive purposes. After this material has been thus introduced, the vital property, sensation, enables the fact of such presence to be known to the instinct, which in its turn superintends and makes useful the involuntary, contractility, in connection with physical principles, to inaugurate physiological proceedings, — that is, to transform said nutritive material into part and parcel of the tissues of the living human organism.

It is not necessary to trace such application in detail as applied to physiological functions, but sufficient only to connect the underlying principles implied in such functions, with the execution of physiological proceedings. Provided the sensibility has by accident introduced within the stomach some kind of foreign material (material not of possible use for constructive purpose; for instance, lobelia), the vital property, sensation, in connection with instinct, discovers such fact, and employs the involuntary, contractility, to execute the act of emesis, — thus illustrating that the vital property, instinct, has the ability to correct some of the errors of sensibility; and also that instinct presides over all material that has found its way into the human organism, using nutritive and eliminating foreign.

All material of every kind, when introduced within the human organism, is subject to such disposal by the involuntary vital properties as its true relation requires.

Instinct, without the aid of sensibility or will, directs many acts of self-preservation and defence. Such proceedings are said to be something that "Nature has done," in distinction to what is presumed, in accordance with the old plan, that some other agency might do. Vital force — in other words Nature — does it all. Material does not act, and is without active principles; the vital principle does the acting. And it may act spontaneously for self-defence, or from invitation, by supplied medicinal relation. When invited by medicine, it is Nature — the active vital principle — which acts. Medicinal contact causes a sensation, to which instinct responds with an involuntary act. The vital property, instinct, superintends all the involuntary doing; and no other agency exercises operative relations with the affairs of organic life in health and disease.

The functions of sensibility and instinct may be independent of each other in certain affairs, but not in all affairs. Sensibility must furnish instinct with the material for constructive purposes; and when properly constructed, those premises are made to exist, — which make it possible to exercise the function of sensibility.

With the conditions of disease, the instinct directly superintends and directs the activities of disturbance, although in many cases sensibility can to a limited degree indirectly guide, with more or less moderation, many of those actions. The use of medicine in its practical relation affords the supply of a contact-cause for moderating and diverting the actions of the instinctive vital agency, — thus enabling us to effect the guidance of those actions which instinct superintends, and vital force operates. Vital force is the active agent that operates the functions of the vital properties, while those vital properties superintend the voluntary and involuntary complex operations of human life. We cannot, however, recognize vital force as an agency independent of those functions.

Medicine has no "active principles" of operative influence within itself; but its presence may be a cause which may occasion the involuntary active vital principle to act differently. Thus we may indirectly cause, to a limited extent, such involuntary vital activity as is thought best to have executed under the existing circumstances. This theory may be illustrated in making use of ipecacuanha to cause a sensation of nausea, which sensation appeals to instinct, to make operative that involuntary contractility which ejects the contents of the stomach. One simple problem understood is as instructive as a thousand similar problems.

A very important practical idea to be kept in view, in guiding the active vital principle, like the guiding of an unruly horse, is to

begin to guide early, before the animal becomes violent and unmanageable. Have in
mind the nature and methods of the operative
vital principle, and thus anticipate results,
and seek to out-general those dangerous
instinctive actions by an early guiding.
There may be as great display of skill in
preventing severe sickness as there is in
curing severe sickness, and the risk for the
patient is much less. Such practice, however, is not always appreciated; and of the
physician employing it this may very likely
be said: "I hardly know how much skill Dr.
Blank has really got. He does n't seem to
have so many very sick patients; and I don't
know how he would succeed with the more
severe ailments."

It is true that while instinct presides
directly over all involuntary acts, sensibility
may to a great degree preside indirectly over
the functions of instinct.

Before proceeding further, it is important
to recognize the distinction between physio-

logical and pathological vital acts, not alone in appearance, but in principle. In other words, What constitutes physiological action? This question seems simple enough at first, but it will be found that much confusion prevails in the department to which it applies.

We shall define physiological action to be the action of the involuntary active vital principle acting in relation to nutritive material for organic constructive purpose, and for the elimination of normal waste and worn-out tissues. We shall define pathological action to be vital action acting in relation to surplus nutritive material not of possible use at the time, and to foreign material.

Physiological action and pathological action are both made operative by the active vital property, instinct, exercised for unlike purposes. There is a dividing line of fact distinction, and there should be a dividing line in ideal distinction; and such distinction should be recognized as among the primary principles which may enable us to solve more complex problems.

In accordance with the other plan, — the accepted plan, on which theories are based, — it is recorded in current and approved medical literature that agencies not vital may execute, and "act physiologically" as well as pathologically.   Thus there is a great distinction between the fundamental premises of the two alleged plans for the development of a medical education.

All readers of medical journals are frequently informed that "Dr. Blank has discovered a new isomeric compound, of which it seems that the differently placed atomic radicals may account for the creation of that new active principle which enables such chemical compound to act physiologically." This is not a stray isolated paragraph; such paragraphs are abundant; and such "discoveries" have been more frequent of late years, as every reputable medical journal will bear witness.

Now, this is a curious state of ideal affairs, although it is alleged science, that human dexterity in the chemical laboratory may be able to produce inorganic compounds "creating" active principles which have the power to transform nutritive material into living human tissues. The intelligent physician has said in reply with much emphasis: "No one entertains any such idea." While such denial is true, no doubt, it may be very difficult sometimes to determine what the idea really is that finds expression in such language. Provided, however, that the accepted plan and theory of alleged medical science is correct, such an idea is rational, not requiring denial; and the profession should continue to insist upon the doctrine that chemical combinations may create "active principles" that have the ability to transform nutritive material into living tissues. The accepted plan and theory of medical science, as now taught, implies that agencies not vital may act physiologically as well as pathologically and medicinally. In fact, the ideal utility of the medical department is founded on the presumption that it is possible to supply an " active principle " and power, not vital, that may temporarily act in substitution of the vital power. Notwithstanding that while this accepted theory has a stronger hold on the imagination than the ancient ideal earth-centre of a former period, and against which the dignity of culture has ever enjoined silence, its supporters have little or no pride in its intellectuality. They do not like to talk about it as a principle, but laud its operative effects. It prevents a mental vacuum, however, and subserves the interests of business as a temporary bridge for the freighting over of unintelligible ideas, constituting the only idea on record of the relation of medicine to the living human organism.

The medical profession does not take kindly to new theories in substitute for old.

They think they need more practical facts, not theories. Such is not true. It is a theory that can be demonstrated, that will contribute most to the advancement of medical science even practically. What is needed at the present time is a theory that will afford a correct idea of the nature of every form of disease, and how produced, — the nature and law of the operating active vital principle, which is ever present in each case and at all stages of the disease; also a correct idea and comprehension of the relation of medicine to the human organism. Neither of these departments at the present time are even claimed in medical literature to be within the grasp of comprehension. Correct theory holds the same relation to a scientific medical practice that the mariner's compass holds to the ship's sailing master: it is a guide for the management of the craft. And while the medical profession abjure the value of theory, and call for facts, they are perpetuating a culture of the most absurd and dangerous theory that ever wrought misery and destruction to a civilized people.

The fallacious medical theory of professional adoption, and the contagious low ideal of medical science which pervades the nonprofessional mind, enable medicine merchants quickly to become millionnaires at the expense of ignorance and unimproved invalidism, and allow ignorance to compete with intelligence in the treatment of the sick, being responsible also for charlatanry and the medical robberies in this age of civilization. Intelligence does not count for much with many sick people. It is the wonderful curative medical agency of discovery which does the business, and which is entitled to the highest consideration. Thus it is of minor importance from whose hands it may be supplied.

It is claimed in medical literature that the " active medical principle " in certain doses will act medicinally, while a larger dose will act pathologically.   It will be illustrated later that the action implied in the *modus operandi* of medicines and the alleged action of poisons are but different degrees in violence of pathological vital action.   There is no medical scientist who can define the difference between a medical action and a pathological vital action ; nor the difference between pathological vital action and the action called disease.

In the study of the science of numbers, we first learn the numerals, multiplication table, and the first four operative principles in mathematics, before attempting the solution of higher and more profound problems.   It is similar with the study of the vital agency : primary premises must engage primary attention.   Unless one becomes familiar with the operative relations of the four ultimate vital properties, and recognizes that such ideal is verified in the affairs of the human organism, it will be impossible to recognize and escape from that calamitous infliction of inheritance

thrust upon civilization in the name of an
"active medical principle." The Ptolemaic
theory of astronomy prevailed for thirteen
hundred years without a record of protest.
The doctrine of an "active medical principle,"
an alleged agency not vital, has been accepted
since the days of Acron, dating back to near
the beginning of the Christian era, and is
equally as fallacious.

Medical literature constitutes a vast store-
house of valuable and practical facts, but
confesses ignorance of the nature, method,
and laws of the vital force which creates
such facts, — alleging that some other agency,
not vital, is concerned in their production.
It alleges also that it is "impossible in the
present state of science to come to any positive conclusion in regard to the nature of the
vital force." But there is no other nature to
vital force except what is implied in the functions of the separate ultimate vital properties and their co-operative relations. What
they do is their nature. It is impossible to

go behind each represented special vital
property, and comprehend any division or
factor of previous existence from which such
special alleged ultimate vital property might
grow. We must be content, for the present
at least, to begin with the nature of such
functions; and just what such functions
execute, constitutes its nature. Physiological action is health-producing action; and
pathological action is disease-producing action.
Disease and pathological vital action represent
a similar disturbance in its essential nature.
Functional disease is pathological vital action;
while organic disease is a construction developed by pathological vital action.

Nature's methods have always been slow
of recognition, constituting a department of
inquiry that is liable to experience erroneous
pre-conceived ideas of the situation, — a situation more difficult to overcome, many times,
than a demonstration of the reality. The pro-
jector of the correct ideal centre of the solar
system had nothing to fear from intellectual

influences; it was the illiteracy of the unscientific mind that developed the unpleasant surroundings. Every department of Nature is presented in accordance with some divine plan; and we allege that the fundamental principles of the Science of Vital Force exist in the functions of the four ultimate vital properties, which must be recognized and verified in support of the elucidation of the more complex problems of animated human life.

4

IV.

ULTIMATE VITAL PROPERTIES.

IT is not our purpose to present an exhaustive treatise of each department, but a more extended mention than was presented in a previous chapter. We shall, however, endeavor to illustrate each division sufficiently to establish a recognition that may be confirmed by affidavits of Nature's testimony.

It may be asked whether it is reasonable to anticipate that the theory and science of vital force will ever be adopted and become *practical?* In reply we can only say that the new plan and science of astronomy was adopted after several generations of protest; and it is as reasonable to anticipate that all correct theories of natural science will be adopted when the human mind outgrows its super-

stitions of ancient origin, and gives reason
a chance to develop. There are some things
in Nature very difficult to ignore: a person
may attempt to ignore the fact that he ever
had a parent; but such doctrine would be
attended with no less difficulty than the
effort to ignore the science and practical
utility of the vital agency. Like mathematics, this science is eminently practical
when understood, and indispensable in aid of
a life-saving treatment of disease, and is
certainly of some satisfaction as an intellectual accomplishment.

Sensibility. This vital property includes
all and every department of intelligence;
and in calling attention to this property of
human life operations, we shall divide the
subject into two grand divisions, — with one
of which all readers are familiar, while the
other remains more or less obscure, with
here and there a recognized out-cropping.
And while each of the two grand divisions
belongs to the department of intelligence,

they seem to emanate from unlike conditions.

Ordinary methods of expressing intelligence will be considered as a *supraliminal*
consciousness; while the phrase "subliminal
consciousness" is recognized as most appropriate in representation of that more obscure
function of mind property and intellectual
ability.

The supraliminal consciousness — above
the horizon, and within the limit of recognition — constitutes the ordinary voluntary
ability of mental function. It is a property
or function of mental ability, which no one
individual mind can measure, and of greater
dimensions than its own circumference;
while the boundaries of this function will
ever remain undetermined. Not only has
this life property the ability to exercise its
function in relation to all the external affairs
of the universe; but it may operate directly
the ultimate vital property, contractility,
and indirectly guide, to a limited degree, the
vital property, instinct.

There is implied in this vital property, sensibility, an ability to originate ideas and to experience emotions of grief, joy, hope, reverence, and to exercise reason and develop a comprehension of those operative principles of Nature which give variety to the visible universe. The special application we are to make of this function and division, as applicable to our subject, will be largely to illustrate its existence in distinction from other ultimate vital properties, and its co-operation in association with other life properties. Sleep is implied in a complete temporary suspension of the active property, sensibility, — a condition from which we may be awakened in various ways, and frequently by the vital property of the individual sensation.

In adopting a name for the obscure division of this mind property, the most advanced thinkers have coined the phrase "subliminal consciousness," as best expressive of an intelligence manifested unlike the ordinary consciousness, — an intelligence uprising, as we might say, from a submerged strata of individual personality. And it has been asked, "Is there some pattern in the very fabric of our nature which begins to show when we scratch the glaze off the stuff?" It may be impossible to define where supraliminal consciousness leaves off, and subliminal intelligence begins; but such, at least, is not our purpose. We only desire to call attention to this department in order to illustrate that there is an obscure feature of human intellectual personality of continued increasing complexity, — a kind of intelligence emanating from our obscure selves, of mysterious operation, not easy of comprehension, and for purposes not wholly recognized.

We can no better illustrate this department than by mentioning some of the operations thus executed. What is called "automatic writing" consists of a written intelligence from some source, of whose nature and purport the writer's conscious intelligence may have no knowledge, and which is sometimes called "trance writing." The operation implied in a genuine "trance" is an illustration of the exercise of a faculty of subliminal consciousness. This singular ability may be exercised in the dark in such feats as landscape and portrait painting.

This sub-state called "subliminal consciousness" belongs to and is a part of the nature of every individual, existing to a more or less degree; and it is capable of being brought to the surface by a system of cultivation. It is not a consciousness which has been acquired through the culture of supraliminal abilities, but a kind of innate consciousness which may acquire intelligence by an entirely different method, — a consciousness which may possess wonderful faculties even in persons whose ordinary intelligence may be mediocre and even below par, illustrated frequently in mathematical and musical "freaks," so called. It is not unreasonable to suppose that much of the most brilliant genius of historic mention may have been found in persons capable of drawing on this quality of highly endowed natural ability. For this subliminal consciousness, with some individuals, has the ability of silent communication. In other words, the subliminal consciousness of A may learn of the subliminal consciousness of B what might be known to B by his supraliminal consciousness. Thus A may learn the thoughts and facts known only to B, — which is often accomplished in test proceedings, and is called "telepathy." The supraliminal mind may imagine itself, and really be, on any part of the globe, while the subliminal may have even a greater ability: it may describe accurately the things seen; it may enter the residence of persons miles away, and describe all there is in the room as correctly, in many instances, as an individual presence might accomplish. Such feats are called "clairvoyance;" and clairvoyance consists in a temporary suspension of the supraliminal mind, and the exercise of the subliminal abilities.

Hypnotism consists in a temporary suspension of the supraliminal faculties of A, while the supraliminal consciousness of B becomes operative with both the thoughts and voluntary mechanism of A; and when complete, the voluntary mind of B, with a good subject, may cause hypnotic A to speak the thoughts of B, while A is not conscious of thus doing.

But how is this done? The explanation, we fear, would be as difficult as to explain how we think.

In the exercise of the subliminal faculties it is possible that A may speak or write a foreign language wholly unknown to A in his normal condition, it being the native language of B. Thus A may know through the subliminal consciousness of B the language which B speaks, and may write a message in that language relative to which B has knowledge, while A may have no knowledge of the language or of the incident mentioned in the message. When a child or an untutored individual goes into a trance,

uses the subliminal faculties, and writes in a
language unknown to his normal consciousness, the inference is often accepted that the
"spirit" of some distinguished dead person
is using this particular organism to commu-
nicate with the living.   Such incidents, however, are telepathic operations, constituting
a subliminal exchange of intelligence.   The
child's subliminal consciousness is in telepathic communication with the same faculty
of one who speaks such language.

No well-informed person will deny the
existence of the alleged subliminal consciousness.   Neither is it intellectually prudent
to circumscribe the limits and abilities of
such division of intellectual function in living human individuality.   That agency
which has been recognized and given the
name of "psychic force" is a factor of the
subliminal consciousness.   This comparative
recent discovery of an agency, frequently
presented unconsciously through the living
human organism, is receiving much attention

from the most advanced minds in civilized countries; and to mention the many singular and varied presentations of this agency would require more space than we can give to this interesting department.

It may not, however, be considered foreign to our subject to state that a large proportion of alleged departed "spirit manifestations" are implied in phenomena presented by the subliminal consciousness of living individuals. And while it may be true that departed "spirit communication" is possible, we can only say that such kind of fact transcends all our experience, knowledge, and comprehension. We are, however, not capable of measuring what may have been revealed to others in addition to the limits of the living subliminal function.

Instinct. The official function of this vital property consists in presiding over all material that is found within the jurisdiction of the human organism, implied in the transformation and arrangement of nutritive material into assimilated living tissues, and the methods adopted in the elimination of waste and foreign material. Both physiological and pathological proceedings are directed by this vital property, and executed through the joint exercise of this function in association with other vital properties.

Sensibility superintends the voluntary acts, while instinct superintends the involuntary. Each department employs other vital properties to aid in the execution of its own official duties.

Instinct as an isolated function is difficult to illustrate except in general outline, and can best be illustrated in association with other functions. It is to be recognized, however, that instinct is not intelligence; that while it may direct many pathological vital acts conducive to the best interest of the human organism, it may also do the opposite. It may direct the execution of acts seriously destructive, which require to be watched and guided. Thus while instinct may correct many errors committed by sensibility, at the same time sensibility must frequently correct and modify the pathological acts operated by this vital property. It may be said that sensibility is a vital property associated alone with the brain, while instinct pervades the whole organism, having its business office associated with nerve ganglions. Instinct may be recognized as more prominent in early life than sensibility, and die later.

It will be noticed that we have given a different interpretation to the function of instinct than is found to prevail in other departments of literature. Nearly all writers and speakers, in illustrating the function of animal instinct, will refer to the acts of the beaver in building his dam as the most typical and generic act representing its application. The question may arise, whether in its true import, as a representative function of organic nature, instinct can be made to do duty in such dual and unlike application as alleged; that is, as being both representative of an involuntary vital property, and also a quality of limited voluntary ability? When one refers to the lexicons to determine the function of instinct, one will find both voluntary and involuntary acts defined as instinctive functions. Webster defines instinct thus: "Unreasoning impulse in an animal, by which it is guided to the performance of an action without thought of improvement in method." Professor Robley Dunglison's medical lexicon defines it thus: "Inwardly moved; the action of the living principle directing its operations to health preservation. The law of instinct is the law of the living principle." The latter definition supports the function which we have attributed to instinct.

The building of a dam by a beaver is a voluntary act directed by the brain, — the sensibility illustrating a limited degree of constructive ability, although it meets the required wants of the species. The function we recognize as instinct is directed by an involuntary vital property, an involuntary, constructive, preservative, living, active principle. From a scientific standpoint, it would seem in very bad taste to allow the term "instinct" to represent both voluntary and involuntary acts; and in place of defining the instinct of a beaver as illustrated in the construction of a dam, we claim it would be more appropriate to have it apply to the construction of the beaver itself.

That portion of Professor Dunglison's definition, "the law of instinct is the law of the living principle," constitutes a valuable scientific text; and while the "living principle" cannot be represented by instinct alone, neither can instinct be illustrated and understood except in connection with other vital properties as applied to the many affairs of the operations of life. Will some philologist please construct a word to take the place of "instinct," that may represent that innate intelligence which enables the animal creation to exercise voluntary ability for self-preservation ?

Sensation. This vital property will prove very interesting from a practical standpoint. The function of this property consists in making known to both sensibility and instinct all existing conditions and material relations, normal and abnormal. Sensibility relates us to the external world, while sensation relates us to the contact world. Voluntary motion is exercised in response to the will, while involuntary motion is exercised by the dictates of instinct in response to a sensation. It is through the medium of sensation that the sensibility, the consciousness, becomes able to know many of the conditions and existing relations which require attention from that department; it is also the medium through which instinct becomes aware of the conditions and relations requiring attention from that vital property.

The variety of sensations are as prolific

and innumerable as the different kinds and degrees of thought; and the question may arise, What is a sensation, and how is it produced?

In non-professional literature incidents are mentioned causing emotion and commotion, which are erroneously called "sensations," — a usage allowed to prevail because no special distinction has been recognized and defined, between sensation and sensibility as distinct life functions. The term "sensation" represents some kind of feeling experienced from a contact relation with those nerves called the "nerves of sensation." This class of nerves are for no other purpose than to experience sensations caused by some existing relation of contact. There will be mentioned later some special exceptions to this statement. At present we will say that sensibility can exercise its function with relations at all distances, while sensation can exercise its function only at insensible distances. Thus we must recognize a very significant distinction between the functions of those two vital properties.

In illustration of different kinds of sensation we may mention some of those feelings, or sensations, implied in sensational pleasures and miseries, — taste, smell, heat, cold, itching, smarting, sensational irritability undefined, and pain of all degrees, comprising a variety of sensations that may be known by the sensibility. There are very numerous sensations not recognized directly by the mind, but which first have relations to the instinct, and which later, indirectly, are thus known to have had existence. Such are implied in many of the causes of disease, to be illustrated later.

The fact that sensations may be produced by contacts affords opportunity for their development at will. Thus sensibility — in other words, intellect — may learn how to produce any kind of sensation desirable; also how many sensations are produced which are not desirable. Those nerves created for

such purpose are ever on the alert to recognize and experience such sensations as become a part of the conditions of health and
disease. Sensation must be recognized as
an ultimate vital property distinct in itself,
and no factor of any other vital property.
Sensibility is a vital property having a function which may comprehend the universe;
while sensation has no function outside that
part of the universe not implied in a contact
with the living organism.

We insist that an ideal distinction shall
become fixed, relative to the difference between the two functions of sensibility and
sensation. No reader can proceed under-
standingly without first developing such a
recognition. If we refer to the lexicons for
a definition, I fear we shall fail to find a
distinction with a difference. And in the
reading of medical literature it will be
observed that the most distinguished writers
permit sensibility to be manifested by every
part of the external body, from the toes to

the crown of the head. No distinction is recognized between the knowledge of a sensation and the sensation itself. The lexicons define sensibility as "a capacity to feel, — as a frozen limb loses its sensibility." In such an instance the leg has lost its function of sensation, and the sensibility has become aware of the fact.

Consider for a moment what progress could be made with the science of numbers, provided its teachers failed to establish an ideal distinction between the fundamental principles of addition and division. We may acquire certain knowledge independent of the vital property of sensation, while some kinds of knowledge must be acquired through that function. There are certain facts that may become known from two unlike methods. We may perceive through the media of the optic organs, and thus know, that an injury has been done to the external structures; while the sensation called "pain" may also enable such fact to be known. There are

numerous facts, however, of which we have
no means of knowing except by this indirect
way of recognizing the kind of sensation
which has been produced from some contact
cause. There is also another combination
through which we are enabled to know of
facts, unlike either of the two mentioned:
not from sight, not from recognized sensation, but from an act — a visible action —
which instinct has directed, and which is
manifested by an involuntary contractility.
In other words, some cause of disturbance
may exist producing a sensation from contact relating only to the instinct, relative to
which instinct directs activities; and we
become aware of such existing contact and
cause only by a recognition of the pathological vital action. For instance, a person
may swallow some strychnia in disguise,
and in a brief time the instinct has become
aware of such fact through the nerves of
sensation, and has directed involuntary
contractility, — convulsions.

The practical man may despise such fine-spun theories, but he should remember that this kind of incident is continually being presented in the manifestation of active disease, where causes are not recognized to exist until consequences are developed. He should keep in mind also that the cause of disease is not active, but always passive. Health is *physiological* vital action, while disease is *pathological* vital action. Words are originated for the transportation of ideas; and unless the original idea is correct, the term may be misleading.

Medicine is as passive as the cause of disease. It does not act; it has no "active medical property." Medicine is useful as placed in contact with the nerves of sensation, to cause instinct to direct a different involuntary vital action more conducive to a speedy restoration of normal vital function. Thus to be able to use medicine most advantageously, — to be able to seize the immediate opportunity, to know what to do and what not to do, — it is extremely essential that those who superintend the management of disease should be familiar with the Science of Vital Force, the only active agency that is operative in the affairs of health and disease. A passive cause is not an active principle; and Nature's functional methods of co-operation and restorative process are diferent, and of finer calibre, than is implied in the doctrine of medical powers and "active medical principles."

Notwithstanding that some of the theories here presented may seem hair-splitting and unpractical, such is not the fact; and the subject includes those which are much finer, and also eminently practical.

Contractility. This is a vital property of animal strength, manifested in muscular tissues, — a contractile strength which can be measured in pounds. This vital property is as distinct in its function as either of those already mentioned.

The sensibility uses and makes application

of this property for voluntary duties requiring muscular assistance, while instinct
makes use of this property for the execution
of involuntary acts requiring muscular effort.
The heart is operated by instinct; but some
individuals can exercise sufficient will-power
to modify the heart's action.   There may
be degrees of mental emotion sufficient to
suspend completely the heart's action and
to cause death.   The function of respiration
can be exercised by both the sensibility and
the instinct.   This function is performed by
a muscular contraction which lifts the ribs,
draws them upward nearer the chin, — tend-
ing to produce a vacuum, which is prevented
by the inflowing of atmospheric air.   The
muscular contraction and lifting of the ribs
can be executed voluntarily; but when this
action is automatically executed, as in the
ordinary method, carbonic acid and other
material continually accumulate in the
blood, and thus come in contact with certain nerves, causing a sensation, — to which

instinct responds with an involuntary contraction of the muscles, which contraction raises the ribs and enlarges the chest for the ingress of atmospheric air required for vital purposes. Certain waste material is thus eliminated through the lungs, and fresh air is supplied for further use in life functions.

Instinct can exercise muscular contractility with those muscles usually operated by the voluntary abilities, — as illustrated in convulsions caused by strychnia, and also in numerous instances where extreme sensational irritability prevails from various causes. The muscular contortions of a decapitated fowl are exercised by instinct. The squirming of eels and other fish lately killed and subjected to heat, thus causing sensation unknown to consciousness, are responded to by instinct; and also the muscular actions induced by electrical currents in contact with a decapitated human body.

The relative preponderance of this vital property as manifested in different animal tissues is of great degree. There is more contractile strength in the feathered species than in' man, in proportion to their weight; while with some insect life this vital property is developed to a still greater degree. The vital properties, contractility, sensation, and sensibility, are each susceptible of much cultivation.

The vegetable kingdom has similar ultimate vital properties. Instinct, sensation, and contractility in a modified function can be recognized in vegetative organisms, while sensibility constitutes a vital property of animal life. Some of the lower organisms of animal life possess but three of the vital properties. The vegetable organism has the ability to use and transform ultimate elements and chemical compounds into organized vegetation; but animal life forces cannot use and assimilate material existing as ultimate elements and chemical compounds.

Elementary material passes upward into chemical compounds, and later into vegetable organic structures; and it then becomes susceptible of being assimilated into tissues of animal life structures. In return, it goes downward into chemical compounds and ultimate elements. Thus there is a continual change in organic material, upward and downward, from a lower to a higher state of existence and return, — an ever ceaseless change of transformation by the various forces of Nature. All material, to become susceptible of transformation into animal structures, must first be lifted up, and organized by the vital forces of the vegetable kingdom, before it is susceptible of transformation into the living structures of animal life.

This previous and required preparation of animal food material conflicts with the alleged legitimacy of the commercial doctrines of the period, implied in the preparation of chemical compounds to be sold and fed to invalids in the name of "restorative nutrient foods." The vital forces of animal life can transform both organized vegetable structures and animal tissues into their own organism.

V.

FUNDAMENTAL PRINCIPLES IN RELATIONS WITH DISEASE.

IN the study of the Science of Vital Force, we not only recognize the existence of the four ultimate vital properties, but also that sensibility has a conscious and an unconscious division of function, — that is, a supraliminal and a subliminal intellectual ability. Instinct is not such a function of animated life as is generally represented; it is not expressed in a limited degree of voluntary ability, but in the superintendence of an involuntary organic function, relative to the disposal of all kinds of material, both useful and otherwise, that are found within the citadel of life from accident or intention.

All experienced sensations produced by material contacts relate either to sensibility or to the instinct. Some sensations are recognized only by the consciousness; while others relate wholly to the duties of instinct, and are not recognized by the sensibility. This latter division of sensations constitutes a very important subject of primary consideration in affairs of disease and medicinal relations. Both departments of sensation may be abnormal to such degree as to develop pathological vital actions, which in themselves constitute active disease. Those which alone relate directly to instinct are produced by causes which develop consequences, before the causes or the abnormal sensations are known by the sensibility to have had existence. It is this division of abnormal sensations which produces disease so unexpected as to give rise to the remark that "disease has attacked the human system."

In addition to the direct relation of the several vital properties to the affairs of life, there are other approximate or sub-fundamental principles entitled to an early consideration.

We must recognize that each vital property may act in a manner both normal and abnormal. Sensibility may become insane, and instinct may construct pathological anatomy; sensation may manifest persistent irritability, and contractility may be exercised in convulsions. All things being primarily normal, proper food in proper quantity will cause normal sensation; instinct will construct healthy structures, all involuntary contractilities will be normal, and sensibility will entertain rational ideas, and in due time correct the theories now in association with alleged medical science. Sensibility surveys and comprehends the affairs of the universe, and may supply a material cause for sensations both normal and abnormal, which are produced by an existing contact. The kind of sensation revealed to sensibility and to instinct will determine the special duty required from the functions of those departments. Instinct is ever on the alert in co-operation with sensation, inspect-

ing every kind and quantity of material
which becomes introduced by design or accident within the contact boundaries of the
citadel of life, with a view to use or eliminate such material. No agency acts except
the vital. Instinct is a function always at
work, and liable to become belligerent at
any hour; while sensibility has natural
periods for repose and activity.

The present old and accepted plan implies
that all material relations with the human
organism may exist in one of three divisions,
—nutrient, inert, and active. The so-called
inert material constitutes a harmless material
except from quantitive, mechanical relations,
and is not of a kind sufficiently objectionable
in small quantity to require special pathological vital acts for its removal, but may be
eliminated in the ordinary manner without
disturbance of normal function. Active
material so called, both medicinal and poisonous, is a kind of material so seriously
objectionable within the citadel of life that a

special pathological vital act is manifested in relation to its presence. Based on this fact alone, the material is called active, because it causes the involuntary vital function to act. Therefore this material is called a medicine, and is said to possess "active medical properties." This kind of material, however, does not act; it has no "active properties;" but its presence being objectionable, there exists a cause for the involuntary vital power to act differently. A passive cause is not an active principle; and the day is coming when it will be considered as absurd to discover an "active medical property," as it would be now to allege that the sun revolved round the earth. A whip is equally entitled to be accredited with "active principles," because it may be so used as to cause both the voluntary and involuntary life powers to act differently.

The ideal "active medical property" is a doctrine having no better claim for consideration than the ancient ideal motion of the

sun.   It is a vagary of superstition not yet
eliminated, and is supported only by common consent, and repudiated by Nature.   A
small relative quantity of such material is
called a "medicine;" a larger quantity is
called a "poison."   An alleged medical
action is a mild pathological vital action;
and the alleged action of poison is a violent
and dangerous pathological vital action.
Thus in the nature of such material is found
the evidence presented and distorted, like
the sun's motion, in the alleged proof that
any material, simple or compound, may
have "active properties."   In other words, a
medical property is implied in that kind of
material so seriously objectionable as to be
a cause for the disturbance of the involuntary vital force, and a cause for it to act
differently.

We have given the correct interpretation
of an alleged "active medical property,"
which is incontrovertible.   There is no educational or practical advantage to be derived

from such interpretation superior to the alleged functions of the ultimate vital properties, but a great and dangerous disadvantage. The discovery of an "active medical property" has long been presumed to be of great value, while such is but the discovery of a material which the human organism cannot use for constructive purpose, and which requires to be eliminated when introduced within the system by a special pathological vital act. There are many millions of such compounds yet to be discovered.

So far as history contributes to such information, Acron (who lived before Pliny) was the first to apply philosophical reason to medicine. He presented an idea surrounded with such entanglements of appearances that it has ever been difficult to eliminate the delusion, and to grasp the true principles and nature of vital force. There are in this problem appearances as misleading as the apparent motion of the sun. The human mind has corrected that ideal operation;

while a similar misconception relative to the
medical department, based wholly on appearances, continues to be perpetuated and thrust
upon the people in this advanced state of
civilization and culture.

Do not let the idea escape recognition that
medicine becomes useful as a means for a
guiding relation, and not as an active *doing*
relation; that its presence becomes a cause
for the vital force to act differently from what
it otherwise would.   And to guide the involuntary vital force knowingly and most advantageously and safely, it is necessary to have
a distinct and clear idea of its nature, varied
functions, and laws.   Notwithstanding that
medical literature has always supported and
persisted in the theory that the "active
medical property" acts, yet when this doctrine is hard pushed for an explanation of
what is meant by the use of such phraseology,
it is not claimed that medicine has a power
to impart, or that it really acts or exercises
a function, — as the words "active medical

property " would seem to imply. Thus while
an active vital property acts, an alleged
"active medical property " does not act.

It is claimed in explanation that medicine
only "makes an impression," in response to
which the active vital principle acts. Such
explanation is very near to being correct,
although it is presented as diplomatic logic
to escape the charge of accepting a medical-
power agency. At the same time, the literature of medical journals makes use of the
terms "medical power," "powerful medicine," and "active medical properties," without any attempt to explain that medicine
has neither power nor active principles to
impart, as would be true if medicine only
"makes an impression."

The inference is not yet disposed of that
the "active medical property " "makes an
impression " in place of acting, and is thus
entitled to be represented as an active medical principle. It is necessary to understand what constitutes a medical impression.

An impression is not a something *done*, but a something *recognized* as done.   It is not unlike a sensation; indeed, the term "impression" is ambiguous, while the term "sensation" is precise, correct, and scientific.   Medicine does not *make* a sensation, but *causes* a sensation.   By simply changing the words "making an impression" to "causing a sensation," the correct fundamental principle implied in the relation of medicine will be represented.   This slight change in phraseology gives an entirely different idea of the source from which the operating active principle is supplied.   In the implied difference of the two statements there is made to exist a pivotal idea as significant as would be a reply to the question, "Which orb is the centre of the solar system, the earth or the sun?"

A distinguished medical writer has said "that medicine acts like the cause of disease."   This is a correct comparison of facts; but the underlying principle that gives existence to such facts fails of being lifted up for recognition. In such an expression the idea is still perpetuated that some mysterious agency or "active principle" is in association with the cause of disease and with medicine which enables each to be active. In other words, some active principle, not vital, is presumed to operate the organs of the living human system. The fact is that the contact of the cause of disease and the contact of medicine each cause a sensation; and one kind of cause is succeeded by a pathological vital action which constitutes active functional disease, while the other kind of cause of sensation is succeeded by pathological vital acts of a different kind, called medicinal effects. Neither has acted, but each has caused a different vital act.

It may be instructive here to refer to authorities that accept the old plan as a basis for theories, and I will quote from a standard publication of 1844 the definition then given by Dr. Wood to medicine: —

"What are medicines? They are substances capable of producing as an ordinary result, and by their own inherent power, certain modifications of the vital functions, which render them applicable to the cure of disease."

Doubtless no one will question the assertion that the time has been when medicine was accredited with having "power." The late Dr. Edward H. Clark, when professor of Materia Medica in Harvard Medical School in 1865, said to his class in a lecture on the subject of Ergot: —

"The same preparation of ergot often acts finely for a period, but may lose its power, or it certainly seems to, although the bottle has remained corked and properly cared for. And how that power escaped, or why it ceased to act, is a problem which will wait till medical science can explore deeper those mysteries which surround us."

Another distinguished writer and medical authority says: "We know very little of the essential nature of disease, — indeed, nothing at all."

Now, functional disease is pathological vital action, — a kind of action and disturbance that cannot be made to exist without a previous abnormal sensation. Thus disease begins with an abnormal sensation. The nature of every involuntary vital act is modified and determined by the kind, degree, and quality of sensation produced. The entire contact world is related to the living human organism only through the vital property sensation. There is no active principle, not vital, that may exercise influence to modify vital function. The modifying principle exists in the character of the sensation. Every kind of material has a causing relation when in contact, which causes some kind of sensation. Food material in proper quantity causes a normal sensation, which is succeeded by a physiological vital action constituting health. That material which may cause disease first causes an abnormal sensation, relative to which instinct directs pathological vital action, — another name for the existing condition called disease. What is called " operative medical action " is a vital action exercised relative to some kind of *sensation*, produced by the contact of material medicine. Thus the actions of the involuntary vital organism for the manifestation of health or disease are dependent on the kind of sensation which is made, allowed, or does exist. The nature of disease is implied in the relation of cause and effect. The cause occasions an abnormal sensation; and the effect is produced by a pathological vital action. This constitutes all that may be implied in "the essential nature of disease."

The vital property sensation is a pivotal life-function of great significance; and while the dictionaries and medical literature fail in outlining the distinction between this vital property and sensibility, it is the first operative function in the affairs of the involuntary living organism. Health, disease, and medical effects are each dependent on the kind of sensation produced. The involuntary vital organism is implied in sensation, instinct, and action. The sensation is a primary manifestation of a single vital property, while the action is a compound function of instinct and contractility. The human organism can execute physiological and pathological vital actions at the same time, — the greater proportion being the former, the less the disease; the greater proportion the latter, the more severe the disease.

The relation of the entire materia medica to the human organism is implied in two grand divisions. First, medicine may cause a sensation without a subsequent development of involuntary action; and second, it may cause a sensation of a degree that is succeeded by the exercise of an involuntary vital action. Thus medicine may cause a sensation only, or it may cause a sensation that will be succeeded by vital action. The cause of disease has precisely similar relations. Disease may exist as a disagreeable sensation, and also as a pathological vital action.

There is only one method possible enabling the voluntary ability, the intelligence, to call up, harness, and guide, and make operative, the involuntary vital force; and that method is implied in making a contact application that will produce and cause sensations. There will be a slight and limited exception made to this statement in a future chapter. The genius of man has enabled him to harness the forces of gravitation, chemical and electric agencies, to fulfil desired results; but the harnessing of the involuntary life force of the human organism, — that department which produces health and disease, — and the calling of this agency into activity at will, has ever remained an unsolved theoretical problem.

The Science of Vital Force affords a lookout station of very different standpoint from that adopted and occupied at the present time. It illustrates the importance of going back to primary principles, recognizing the difference of relation between an "active" and a passive cause of disease, between an alleged "active medical property" and a passive medical cause of sensation. It illustrates that the cause of disease is no more active than a bowlder on a railroad track is active in a railroad accident. The cause of disease is *material in the wrong place*, thus interfering by its presence with the normal function of an agency which is wholly separate from the cause of the disturbance.

Based on the foregoing alleged fundamental principles, another very important question arises: What constitutes the varied causes of abnormal sensation? It would be neither possible, practicable, nor instructive to enumerate all such causes, while it would be of interest to consider the unlike divisions that may include a great multiplicity of such causes.

Division A. In this division may be included food material undigested and in excess of required use, retained waste material, and chemical compounds that have formed from such material, — all of which may require special pathological vital acts for their removal.

Division B. This will include all kinds of foreign material, organic and inorganic; filth material, solid, fluid, or gaseous, swallowed or inhaled; simple elements and chemical compounds introduced as such, and chemical products of the same of later formation, — all of which constitute primary causes of abnormal sensation, followed by a disturbance later, authorized by the vital property instinct, which presides over all material having a contact relation.

Division C. This may include mechanical causes of many kinds, implied in lacerations and compressed nerve structures, and also extremes of heat and cold from external associations, — all of which may cause primary abnormal sensations, liable to be succeeded by pathological vital actions.

Division D. This will comprise secondary causes, — a very large factor of disturbance ever being developed within, after the diseased process once begins from any primary cause. This class of causes includes local congestions, mechanical compressing of nerve tissues, development of higher temperatures of the blood (a secondary cause liable to produce prolonged and serious consequences later), morbid pathological products and infiltrations developed by diseased action, and chemical changes that take place with such material within the organism.[1]

[1] There is no kind of disease that may be known by any special name, which has its beginning and total cause for continuance implied in a relation of primary cause. This is an important fact for practical consideration, as well as an indispensable recognition in support of the theory of cause and effect, as presented in the operative procedures by the involuntary life force in the various forms and complications of disease.

The secondary causes, produced by pathological disturbance and chemical changes, — causes developed within, — are of serious significance, which are made to exist more or less each day. Primary causes are frequently of minor consideration when compared with the secondary, which are later made to prevail. Primary causes may often be removed, and yet the disease continue from causes later developed, which many times are very difficult to control. Blood poison in most cases is implied in products developed within, from some disturbance of a primary cause, which would be harmless to some, while fatal to others. Different organisms develop secondary causes in a very dissimilar manner.

Causes of disease first produce abnormal sensations, which may be known sometimes by both sensibility and instinct, and may receive attention from either or both, while at other times abnormal sensation is recognized only by instinct. Consciousness may

infer, and in fact know, that such an incident has occurred, not from a recognition of
the sensation as a pain or any other kind of
sensation, but from a recognition of some
involuntary active disturbance, — a disturbance which could not occur without a previous abnormal sensation from some cause.
This may be illustrated in the incident of
swallowing strychnia in disguise, as well as
in many cases of disease where the consequences are recognized before the primary
cause is known to exist. In a very large
variety of diseases we recognize the consequences, the disturbance, before we are in the
least aware that causes exist.

Among the fundamental principles there
is another distinction to be recognized, which
is of great importance both because of theoretical and practical relations, — that while
abnormal sensations may be followed by
pathological vital actions called disease,
there may be numerous abnormal sensations
that are *not* succeeded by pathological vital

actions. This class of ailments are called "nervous" diseases, constituting a kind of trouble existing as disagreeable sensations, from which the person or patient seeks relief. In close connection and corresponding with this existing condition, there may be recognized also that with medicinal relations there are kinds and small quantities of medicine which only occasion sensations that may be agreeable or otherwise, and which are not succeeded by any visible or recognizable active medicinal effects.

Not only is there a theoretical but also a practical value to be associated with such facts. Thus the condition called "nervous" disease, and the fact that an agreeable sensation may be produced with medicine; it becomes rational to infer that the temporary treatment of many of those disagreeable feelings consists largely in swapping sensations, — in producing a more agreeable sensation in exchange for the disagreeable. And while this suggestion seems consistent as a theory, the practical facts seem to verify the utility of such application. It is in harmony with the defined functions of the vital properties, and with the theory of medicinal relations. For instance, an intolerable itching of the skin may frequently be relieved with a two-grain solution of *Hydrargyri bichloridum* to one pint of boiling water, — the quantity of bichloride being only sufficient to effect a swapping of sensations, and not sufficient to cause an abnormal sensation to a degree that will be responded to by instinct with a series of involuntary activities. Hunger and weariness are both sensations that may often be relieved by a cup of strong tea, and also by alcoholic spirit. The person thus relieved is liable to infer that such remedy has contributed nutritive support and energy to his organism. The craving sensation in alcoholism is being treated by supplying a cause for a different sensation, — in other words, a swapping of sensations. Patients often request their physician to give them a tonic, some "bracing" medicine that will relieve the tired feeling and build them up. This is not the place to discuss to what degree such a practice may be admissible; but it may here be said that such practice is liable to insure a profitable patient for the physician, and in many instances it would be like attempting to cure alcoholic spirit consequences with alcoholic spirit medication.

This branch of medical practice implied in the swapping of sensations, regardless of correct regimen and proper surroundings of sanitary relations, constitutes a serious impediment to the welfare of invalids. It is encouraged by the experience of a more agreeable temporary sensation, and supported by the accepted, fallacious, and dangerous theory of "active medical properties." The new sensation is given the interpretation of a supplementary "active principle," which is presumed and alleged to be a contribution of temporary energy that is doing something to help Nature. Consequently there are levied millions of tribute on the prevailing ignorance of the science of recovery, and the standard of national health is being thus seriously impaired.

The term "medical tonic" is an ideal misnomer. All kinds of alleged medical tonics — quinine, ale, and beer — are but so many kinds of material that effect a temporary exchange of sensations. This is a subject worthy of the consideration of philanthropists, and of all who may have an interest in the general welfare of the individual and the nation. Medical tonics and "bracing" medicines are made useful in that commercial transaction implied in the swapping of sensations. The patient mistakes the exchange of sensations for a contribution of energy; and the physician often makes a similar mistake in giving his patient chemical compounds as alleged constructive material. When a person feels that a medicine has given him strength, the fact is that only a different sensation has been produced.

Thus *feeling* less weary, they infer they have more strength. But the effecting an exchange of sensations with such material is no more an evidence that constructive nutrient material has been supplied to the body, than the excitement produced by a new idea is evidence that a contribution has been made for the support of brain weariness.

A multitude of *alleged* "nerve foods" and "nerve-tonic" compounds belong to this class of medicines, although such are not foods. Alcoholic spirit is the old "stand-by" remedy for weariness, antedating all other discoveries. An eminent medical writer says, "There are conditions in which alcohol acts simply as material for the production of force, and may be looked upon as a food which requires no digestion, and sets free in a useful form its latent energy." On the contrary, it has no "latent energy," and does not "produce force;" but is a cause for a new sensation and the expenditure of vital energy in a different direction. The United

States Dispensatory and mouth-piece of legal-tender ideas is permitted without protest to continue imparting the information that "alcohol in a diluted state gives additional energy to muscles and temporary exaltation to the mental faculties." With such doctrines emanating from the highest accredited institutions of learning, it is not strange that mankind should resort to the practice of drinking alcoholic spirit for the "energy" it may be presumed to supply, — a doctrine apparently supported by an experience of "*feeling* better."

As a people and a nation we are living in an age of cultured and singular delusion, — a delusion which is inflicting consequences that are sought to be abolished without an effort to correct the cause. The cause is the false education. People drink alcoholic spirit to enable them to "*feel* better," and to give them strength; and they do this in accordance with the doctrines of alleged and accepted science. While the would-be

benefactors of the race are trying to avert
the miseries thus produced, by resorting to
prohibitive legislative enactments, would it
not be equally as beneficial, to say the least,
to give special attention to an education that
would cease to develop and perpetuate such
expectancies? There are many people who
have not the ability to deal safely with a
practice implied in such fallacious expectancies of supplied energy; and while the
highly cultured frequently stagger under such
responsibilities, they should have pity in
place of censure for those who are less
capable.

A most successful medical practice for the
saving of human life must be implied in such
methods of guidance of the vital energies as
will occasion the least expenditure of capital
stock of the existing vital force. Medicine
does not supply temporary "active principle" or medical power, but it occasions vital
energy to be expended in a different manifestation. The practice of medicine without

a knowledge of the nature and laws of involuntary vital force is frequently a dangerous experiment, quite similar to the guiding of a ship in a storm without a mariner's compass. And when the people awaken to the importance of this branch of education, there will be a simultaneous effort by all cultured civilization to dissipate the fog of superstition and ignorance which is consigning thousands annually to an untimely grave.

In the development of an enlightened civilization, numerous ideal fallacies of Nature's plans and methods require to be eliminated. The ideal flat earth had to be abandoned; the human mind had to outgrow its ideal associations relative to inorganic material transformation, and surrender the expectancy that base metals could be changed to gold; the popular idea of the centre of the solar system had to be changed, which was effected under protest and much remonstrance. It is said, however, that such crude ideas prevailed

before the star of science had illuminated
the pathway of the human mind, during the
dark age of superstition. But the combined
crudities of thought relative to all those
departments of science do not out-weigh in
magnitude the present calamitous fallacy
that presumes and accepts the existence of
some agency in Nature, not vital, which
acts on the human organism to produce
disease, and also some agency and "active
medical principle" which acts to operate the
organs of human life, supposed to possess a
curative influence to restore health. History keeps green the ideal fallacies of the
past, while the worse and dangerous ideal
fallacy of to-day remains unchallenged. The
expectancy that an "active medical property" has existence, that it can be bottled,
sold, and used as a contribution of temporary
energy in substitution for vital force, has as
strong a hold on human credulity as any of
the ancient delusions that were accepted on
the basis of appearances. Facts warrant

the use of stronger epithets than any here employed, and which will surely be found in future history, relative to this period and age of experimental research for the discovery of an imaginary substitute for vital force.

VI.

DISEASE GERMS.

THE modern germ-theory of disease implies that diseases, more or less, may
be caused by germs, — which theory constitutes a subdivision of alleged causes that is
entitled to separate consideration.   Its advocates say that it is a subject "entitled to
coolest criticism, — never leaving, however,
the experimental facts for the airy region of
wild theorizing and speculation."   We do
not care to deny "facts," but desire to learn
what *kind* of fact is determined by such
experiment.   Every fact in Nature is entitled
to an explanation; and whatever theory is
presented for that purpose may be called
"wild" or rational according to the standpoint accepted by the observer, according to

which lookout station is occupied, — the old plan or the new.

The germ-theory is a doctrine alleged to be based on facts, of a kind however that will be mentioned later. It has been projected to "account for the methods of multiplication of dangerous disease." Disease as considered in the light of the germ-theory, called the "ravages of parasites," and considered also in the light of the old plan and according to the interpretation of distinguished authorities, is said to "attack" the human family, and "pursues the ordinary routes of travel, following the human race along ocean paths." According to this quotation from an article on the germ-theory found in a journal of acknowledged scientific authority, it would seem that disease chooses to inhabit regions frequented by the human family!

We must begin the consideration of the "germ-theory of disease" by changing the language of the text, — making it to read, "germ-theory of the *cause* of disease." There-fore it will be important to determine to what extent an alleged germ may be a cause of disease, — which constitutes all there is to consider of alleged "facts" implied in such discovery, and also constitutes the *kind* of fact we propose to examine. In a previous chapter we disposed of the relation of the cause of disease to the human organism; and whatever relation an alleged "germ" may have, it can be of no different relation as a "multiplier of dangerous disease." The *cause* of disease does nothing; it has no influ-ence, it is not active; it is only a cause of abnormal sensation.

What does the word "germ" signify, and what is a germ?

It is important to go to the bottom of this germ-theory. A germ signifies that which is to develop into something, and from which something has its origin. The micro-organism which constitutes the alleged germ may be a microscopic plant or an animalcule.

Those organisms feed on organic matter, seizing it on its downward course from a previous higher organization; and thus they multiply wherever it is possible to obtain such nutriment for their support. The plant organizations are designated as "baccilli," and the animalcules as "bacteria" and "protozoa." The term "parasite" is given to both, signifying a micro-organism which draws its nourishment from other organisms. The terms "microbe" and "bacteria" are frequently applied to both kinds of organisms; while numerous special names are used to designate some variation of appearance as found in different fluids and localities of the body. The germ micro-organism, of microscopic discovery, does not develop into anything; it remains the same until death. Therefore it is not a germ in that sense of the definition; and there is much doubt, well founded in the nature of things, whether disease, seldom without inoculation by intention, can have its origin from this kind of alleged cause, — that is, from living micro-organisms. Doubtless the alleged germ is sometimes a cause of disease, — that is, a cause of abnormal sensation of a degree sufficient to develop active disease. Such kind of cause, however, has its relation obscured by being called a "germ." This kind of cause is no more entitled to be called a "germ" than are numerous other kinds of primary causes that are not micro-organisms. All kinds of causes have only one kind of relation, — a cause of abnormal sensation, the first existing change in the direction of disease.

The accepted theory of putting the *cause* of disease for the *production* of disease, in accordance with the old plan, supposes the cause to exercise an influence, and to act. It can be demonstrated, however, that a cause of disease does not act, but only constitutes a cause for the involuntary vital force to act abnormally; which in itself is the disease. Thus it would be very difficult to determine what kind of a cause was a germ and what kind not a germ, while all causes have a similar relation.

We thought we had good reason for changing the phraseology "germ-theory of disease" to "germ-theory of the cause of disease;" and we now find also good reason for insisting that in place of the last form of words this subject might be better represented by the phrase "bacterial cause of disease." The word "germ" is wholly out of place in such relation; and should the microscope be applied to the *idea* as well as to the plant and animalcule, the outline would appear very different.

We still have the question before us, Do bacteria cause disease? Is it the nature of such organisms as a dried spanish fly to have an irritant relation to nerve tissues? Were they not designed merely as scavengers? Do such organisms exist most plentifully in a healthy body, or in a body already diseased? Is it not true that such micro-organisms find their best opportunity for existence because some diseased action has previously existed ? Every bacteriologist knows that such is the fact.

Practical facts seem to show in some instances that disease has evidently been produced by the transference of such micro-organisms to a different individual. On the other side is the fact, equally as practical, that such inoculation does not always produce disease. So seldom has disease been thus produced, compared with the failures to produce, that some able physicians have alleged that the germ-theory was inapplicable even upon the basis of experiment. The supposition is not without some reason that micro-organisms, more or less constructed from filth material, might break down and present an amount of poisonous material sufficient to be a cause for vital disturbance in some instances.

In brief, from the basis of fundamental vital principles and rational reason the bacterial cause of disease, without inoculation, would seem so nearly harmless that it would be wiser to recommend the prevention and the destruction of filth material as a sanitary measure, rather than to consider the microbe the cause of disease. Is it not rational to suppose that the material from which the micro-organism is created, would be a less cause of disturbance existing in an organized state than in its previous condition susceptible of solution and absorption ? Who will deny that such micro-organisms do not exercise the function of scavengers ?

The "disease germ" and bacterial cause of disease is considered more applicable to zymotic disease, — that is, those diseases propagated by contact, measles and scarlet fever being illustrative types. The discovery that yeast, or leaven, is a multiplication of microscopic plant organisms, gave rise to the doctrine of the germ-theory of zymotic disease; and the well-known fact that such disease seldom develops more than once in the same individual furnishes theoretical complications in association with the germ-theory that require special consideration. On the supposition that a growth of micro-organisms, more or less, constitutes the cause of such disease, is it not a singular fact that a human organism can develop a *nidus*, or material for such growth, only once in a lifetime, — and especially when we consider that with such disease, when existing, there is a more or less rapid production of poison within the system that is eliminated through the skin, which material also becomes a local irritant at the point of escape ?

Now we ask, is this escaping poison a micro-organism, dead or alive, a broken down product of such life, or is it a poison developed by pathological vital action ? The fact that such disease rarely occurs more than once in a lifetime gives rise to two important questions, — Can the human system develop only once a compound food-material for the growth of micro-organisms ? and, Can pathological vital action develop a second time a similar poisonous product to what was first produced, through tissues that have once been subjected to a diseased action ?   It is a well-known fact that certain tissues can be modified by a diseased action, and prevent a recurrence of effusions through serous membranes.   A cicatrix never has the function of the tissue it has displaced.   Should this subject be considered in its completeness, we think the weight of testimony would favor the acceptance of the theory that pathological vital action could seldom develop more than once the specific poison peculiar to such diseases.   And is it not more rational to accept such a method of supplied cause, — a pathological product, — than to accept the allegation that the human organism cannot more than once in a lifetime elaborate a fluid compound capable of the growth of micro-organisms ?   Should the subject of the bacterial cause of the zymotic group of diseases be carried up to the high court of inquiry, it is reasonable to believe that this group, which is presumed to contribute the most support to the germ-theory, would be found to contribute the least.

This group of diseases, which seldom occur more than once in a lifetime, while subject to the same general laws of cause and effect, is subject to a different production of supplied primary causes not common to other disease. That is, whatever the primary disturbing cause may be, the preponderance of secondary product is similar. In this interesting group of diseases we have to infer that the primary cause is similar to that poison which is eliminated through the skin, which in itself constitutes a cause for local disturbance at its place of exit designated the eruption. Thus we are persuaded to infer that the cause of zymotic disease is a pathological product, and not in the nature of micro-organisms. We have also to consider that some of the zymotic diseases do develop away from all possible contagion as a sporadic presentment; and it is rational to infer that some unlike primary cause, which in itself will not propagate the disease in a different person, may cause a pathological disturbance which will produce this special poison, and that the poison so generously produced will from contact produce a similar disease in one whose system has never been subjected to a previous and similar pathological disturbance.

In accordance with the apparent nature of things, based on natural fundamental principles, it would seem that the micro-organism might be more of a scavenger than anything else, — both the harmless and the alleged disease-microbe. Those scientists who make this subject a study do not claim to find an alleged disease-microbe in a healthy organism, but only where disease already exists, — where there is something for that special variety to feed upon. The micro-organism as found in a healthy human body is regarded as harmless, while the microbe found in a diseased system is charged with being the cause of disease. Why not allege that the harmless microbe may be the cause of health, — the health germ of balanced functional harmony?

Vaccine matter and small-pox virus are pathological products, and with persons who never had such disease this virus will occasion a vital disturbance which will develop a similar product; but when the virus has been changed by chemical agency, its contact relations will not occasion such a vital disturbance as will produce the specific pathological virus. And it may be well to state in this place that the practice of vaccination, and its legitimate and effectual protection against small-pox, is founded on laws of vital processes, which are as stable and capable of demonstration as are the laws which make it possible to calculate an eclipse. Its utility has been demonstrated by experience, while the laws of its applicability and appropriateness are supported by the science of vital force.

The operative laws of vital force in relation to the production of the cause of scarlet fever give equal protection through a similar modification. But the question may arise, whether the bovine species can have scarlet fever; and if so, how we can secure the special pathological product for such purpose. A London physician some ten years ago announced an outbreak of this disease among the cows in that vicinity, — a disease said to be known in veterinary text-books as "erythema mammillarum;" but the process of securing such modified virus has not yet become a matter of record. In connection with the mention of this law of possible utility, we will also say that the treatment of scarlet fever based on the principles of the new plan will prove far more successful.

The precise existing condition of the cause of typhoid fever is yet an unsolved problem in the minds of the profession; and to say that typhoid fever is caused by a "disease germ" conveys but little intelligence on the subject.   We thus have for consideration the question whether such cause is a pathological product, or the product of chemical agency; also whether such disease may be caused from relations of bacterial existence, which are alleged by some German authorities to secrete a virulent poison, and thus make it possible to develop such disease from micro-organisms that have been transferred from a person previously sick with typhoid fever. Material existing as a pathological product is composed of organic elements that are liable to experience chemical changes. Thus when typhoid fever is developed from drinking polluted water, is the material cause a soluble pathological product, or a soluble chemical product?   Or is it neither, but consisting of micro-organisms created in association with previous disease?   There are numerous instances where it appears that persons have contracted typhoid fever from visiting those who were afflicted with this disease. Thus it would seem that the exhaled poisonous vapor from the patient had been inhaled by the visitor. In such instances there may be found strong evidence to support the inference that the cause of typhoid fever exists as a soluble pathological product. This disease has also appeared to develop from surroundings of filth material, and a residence in close relations with a pig-sty.

The complexity of this subject in all its variations is very great; and it is a subject entitled to more attention than we can give space for in this introductory volume.

VII.

TOLERATION.

THIS may be a unique term for the representation of a scientific principle; but in accordance with the dictionary definition, it stands for a useful factor of organic economy, — "the allowance of that which is not wholly approved."

No doubt the thoughtful reader has observed that in the *theory* we have presented, implied in a primal cause of abnormal sensation that wakes up and is succeeded by a pathological vital action, — an action that in itself may develop secondary causes for continued abnormal sensation, and a prolonged continuance of pathological actions,— there is no provision made for the termination of such disturbed vital action. Thus, so far as the theory has been presented, a disturbance

once started goes on forever to the end of
individual life. Therefore, to preserve the
theory and also the patient, and to enable a
return to conditions of health, some other
principle in Nature not mentioned must take
part in disease problems; that is, a cause for
abnormal sensation must be allowed to exist
which is no longer the incentive for a continuance of pathological proceedings. In
other words, we must allow for a principle
permitting causes of a kind that have previously occasioned abnormal sensations to a
degree sufficient to arouse pathological activities, to continue to remain and not develop
such disturbance.

Now, while such a new principle is desirable for the benefit of the patient, and indispensable for the support of the theory
advanced, is there a principle provided in
Nature to meet this practical and theoretical
emergency? In demonstration of such a
provision, we call attention to the well-
known fact that people who reside in a

malarious district sooner or later become "acclimated," as they call it; that is, they become accustomed to the surroundings, and their nervous system tolerates the malarial poison without the development of chill and fever.

All medicines, when long continued, fail to produce the same effect from the same quantity, and are said not to act. The drinker of alcoholic spirit is required to increase the quantity in order to produce the same effect. The *ergot* which was said by the medical professor to have "lost its power" is an illustration of the principle of toleration. Children who are brought up in the tenement houses of a crowded city will tolerate for a long period those causes of disease which would disturb a healthy child from a rural district in a very brief time.

Toleration, then, represents a principle of self-preservation in association with the involuntary function, and oftentimes will compensate for neglect of voluntary duties.

The existence of this kind of principle is too well known to require further illustration. In such a principle there is implied a wise provision of Nature, a reserve corps, for self-preservation under certain circumstances. It is the principle which makes it possible that certain diseases may be self-limited. It is a distinguishing principle existing in acute disease, while not operative in chronic.

Now, while this principle crops out spontaneously in many actions of the human organism, it may also be artificially induced by the physician through medication, from sedative and anæsthetic medicines whose presence in contact with certain nerves abrogates more or less the function of sensation.

The principle of toleration is not a fifth vital property; it is not applicable to physiological proceedings, but applies only, and to a limited degree, in association with pathological actions. It is a principle to be ever kept in mind in the treatment of disease; and it is a condition to be induced under certain circumstances, and not to be induced under other circumstances. Sometimes serious consequences follow upon the transposition of the application of this principle. Thus to be able to guide most advantageously the involuntary active vital principle in conditions of disease, constitutes the most valuable acquisition in the practice of medicine.

Special senses. It might be well in this place to allude to the subject of special senses, frequently called special sensations and sensibilities, as implied in special methods of acquiring intelligence, and recognized in the functions of touch, taste, smell, hearing, and sight.

The first three of these are special sensations, while hearing offers a more complex problem. The transmission of sound being yet in the mill of controversy, — divided up between the undulating wave, the corpuscular, gelatinous luminiferous, and interstellar æther theories, — to what degree and how the function of sensation is involved in it is not yet a settled problem. Sight seems to approximate a special sensibility, the image being produced through physical principles, and perceived by some special function of the brain.

The nerves which experience certain sensations cannot experience different sensations; and it might be truly said that the function of sensation is implied in an innumerable multiplicity of special sensations, some being recognized by the sensibility, while others relate to the vital property instinct. We quote the following from a standard text-book on physiology: "By the sense of touch is usually understood that modification of common sensibility of the body of which the skin is the special seat." It is not possible to understand the science of numbers until a clear idea is made to prevail of the distinction between the primal fundamental principles ; and the same is true of vital-power science. So too the

function of the four ultimate vital properties
must exist in clear ideal outline, before it is
possible to comprehend the nature and co-
operative methods of the vital agency in
affairs of disease.

VIII.

MEDICAL PRACTICE.

IN a medical practice based on the fundamental principles of active vital force, a
different idea of duty will be recognized
from that which is based on expectant
action of presumed "active medical properties." The subject will have an entirely
different appearance from this new standpoint of perception. It is a change *from* an
ideal position, where theories and thoughts
are out of harmony with facts, to a basis
where theories and thoughts will be in harmony with facts and with Nature's plan, and
susceptible of easy demonstration. The
whole field of natural phenomena will take
on as different an ideal appearance as was
effected by the change of the ideal centre of

the solar system.   Facts will be recognized whose meaning will be better understood. There will be recognized indications of what to do; also, which is equally as important, what not to do; also what degree of guidance of vital *agency* should be effected, and when it should be let alone.   The cause of disease will be recognized as passive; and it will also be recognized that disease may exist as an abnormal sensation only, and as a pathological vital action, — and sometimes both. It will be recognized that medicine does not act, nor make impressions, but only causes sensations;   that thus sensations may only require to be exchanged, or other sensations produced of such degree as to be succeeded by pathological vital actions, which will be the new phrase representing medicinal effects in substitution for the *modus operandi* of medicine.   There will be recognized causes of disease both primary and secondary; and the latter often being far more serious in their relations, great advantage will accrue to that method of treatment which will most effectually modify and prevent the development of these secondary causes.

In the illustration of the varied causes of disease, — the causes of abnormal sensation, — we made use of several divisions for such enumeration; and with the subject of applied medication, the same method will contribute better to an illustration of the situation. While medicines may be given to neutralize causes of disease, there are but two grand divisions of medicinal relations with vital functions. One division includes that relation which produces sensations that are not succeeded by pathological vital actions. The other division is represented in that relation where sensations are produced that *are* succeeded by pathological vital actions.

First Division. In treating disease existing only as an abnormal sensation, some kind of bad feeling without active disturbance, the indication is met by making such

application and using such remedy as will
cause a new sensation, — thus swapping sensations, producing an agreeable in place of
a disagreeable sensation.

In attempting to effect such exchange, it
is very important that the kind and quantity
of medicine used shall not produce such
degree of abnormal sensation as to cause a
subsequent pathological vital action to
develop.   The cause both of the development
of active disease and of the development of
active medicinal effect is implied in the production of an abnormal sensation of a degree
that will be succeeded by pathological vital
action.   We have sufficient reason for believ-
ing that great and serious mistakes are often
made in failing to recognize such relations,
and many pages would be required to do
justice to the illustration of such errors.   In
medical practice these errors are numerous
so far as medication is required in the swapping of sensations.   While there may be
numerous abnormal sensations requiring no

other treatment than that of being exchanged for new, there may, on the other hand, abnormal sensations prevail where, instead of *exchange*, some operative proceedings should be instituted for the *removal of the cause.* But while in some instances the cause may be removed, in many cases this is impossible. In such cases a course of hygienic treatment is required, to develop surroundings favorable for normal sensations.

It is this kind of fact, implied in the exchange of sensations, which has made the Homœopathic practice acceptable and scientifically correct in certain cases. The Homœopathic theory, however, is as irrational as other medical theories, — claiming, like the others, the use of " active medical principles " that act similar to the vital principle. In place, however, of administering medicine having "similar powers," the Homœopathic dose has been of a size, that has caused a new sensation, but not of a degree sufficient to develop visible pathological vital actions.

The small dose meets many requirements, but it does not meet all, as experience has revealed even to that school of practitioners.

In referring to "schools of medicine," we may say that all scientific medical practice is based and operative on the nature and functions of vital force. This whole matter of superintending and treating disease is not implied in a *meddling* supervision, but in a *watchful* supervision. There are many compensating methods for the readjustment of normal sensations and normal activities consigned to the custody of instinct. Thus instinct may be doing the best within the limit of possibility, and only requires to be let alone; while at other times instinct may require the exercise of much intelligence — of sensibility — for the safe guidance of its function.

Second Division. This division includes a medical practice in relation to pathological vital actions, — actions induced by primary and secondary causes of abnormal sensation; causes existing as pathological products, chemical compounds, infiltrations, mechanical congestions, and abnormal temperature.

It is not our purpose to advise what to do; but we propose to call attention to some of the relations that may be implied in those operative effects which medicine may have in the production of pathological vital actions. In the treatment of disease, shall we deploy vital action, and thus reduce the violence by dividing the direction of vital action ? This was a method of practice once highly esteemed, and which gave rise to the doctrine of *contraria curantur*, — a method of practice that was called "allopathic," which term is now erroneously used in the place of "regular," to distinguish the first schools of medical practice from the numerous names of modern invention. Shall we seek to diminish the violence of vital action by diminishing the primary and secondary causes ? What kind of causes can be eliminated, and what neutralized; and how can the same be effected? When shall we use sedatives to make causes tolerant, and how shall we reduce abnormal temperature?

Such divisions of treatment are of great practical consideration where one method might prove serious when substituted for the other. What was best to do yesterday, may not be the most useful to-day. Have we done our whole duty in treating conditions as they appear from day to day? Shall we not anticipate severe and serious complications in accordance with the laws of cause and effect, with the nature of vital force? Shall we not seek to outgeneral the production of effects by guiding the vital action differently, and thus avoid what would otherwise be a serious disturbance? In these divisions of treatment there is a wide field for diversity of application, which might be much better illustrated in connection with special disease. Every form of disease is liable to develop some condition peculiar to itself,

with different persons, implied in the relations of primary and secondary causes and
in the nature of operative vital force.

Third Division. This is not a division of
relations, unlike the two already outlined, but
a classification to include and illustrate a few
practical principles slightly removed from an
ultimate fundamental basis, and to be made
operative more in a distinction of methods to
be adopted, and for miscellaneous suggestions
that will be crowded into diminutive space.

Abnormal temperature of the blood, of
high degree, is a secondary cause important
to consider; for too frequently it is the
pivotal cause of complicated disturbance
resulting in death in acute diseases. It is a
cause not always recognized in its true
relation to subsequent events.

How shall we reduce the abnormal temperature of the blood, for the best interests of
the patient? High temperature is sometimes diminished by suppressing vital action

from medication, where such action is producing material for rapid combustion. This, however, is not a safe method in severe cases; for we thus diminish the secondary cause — temperature — at the expense of retaining certain effete material not susceptible of elimination by different process, which should be favored with an early opportunity of escape. High temperature reduced by conduction enables both the early escape of such material, and at the same time keeps the secondary cause — heat — below the maximum temperature of greatest disturbance and danger. The reducing of high temperatures by conduction, from external application of wet compresses, is far more prudent and always within the limit of immediate control. The ratio of deaths from primary causes of disturbance is very small compared with those from secondary development; and among the secondary causes, it is doubtful if any are equal to abnormal temperature of the blood as a death producing complication in acute diseases. At the same time, it is a cause the most easily and effectually controlled, and apparently the least recognized.

Among the numerous causes of disease both primary and secondary, there will exist causes to be eliminated, causes to be neutralized, causes to be made tolerant, and causes with which we can do none of these, — causes that require to be outgeneralled by deploying the vital energies. There are several valuable practical principles that can be illustrated in a case of rattlesnake poison. We have said that small-pox virus was a pathological product, while rattlesnake virus is a physiological product. The effects of rattlesnake virus may often be outgeneralled by the use of a large dose of *spiritus frumenti*, which may apply in various relations. The presence of the medicine causes the nerves of sensation to be preoccupied, and thus to be more tolerant to a certain degree; or, in other words, the medicine has early relation to primary sensation, including more nerve structure. It is of great importance to develop early primary sensations, and thus keep the instinctive department of vital power from acting. It is desirable to have the virus escape recognition from the function of sensation. The medical remedy admits of an early and general diffusion over the entire system, and receives attention by a manifest increase of blood sent to the capillaries of the skin, favoring the elimination of the remedy; at the same time it prevents any severe local disturbance at the point of the inception of poison, thus outgeneralling the early effects of snake poison by the development of a different primary cause of disturbance over a greater and a different region, and giving time for an organic dissolution of the virus into less objectionable relations to living tissues.

Death from rattlesnake virus is due to secondary causes, while strychnia is a primary cause of death, — death ensuing from exhaustion by violent persistent muscular contractility. Hydrocyanic acid is a primary cause of death, through relations to a different vital property, from a paralysis and abrogation of that division of the functional property of sensation which is operative in connecting instinct with executive involuntary contractility.

In this distinction there may seem to arise a very delicate question, — Why not infer that instinct is paralyzed? In reply we say, that after death from such primary cause the galvanic current will occasion an abnormal sensation, irritability, followed by muscular contractions of the extremities, — indicating that only a certain division of the sensational function has become inoperative, while instinct remains able to exercise its function, as in the case of experiments after decapitation.

As this third division is a medley of causes, operations, principles, and facts, we trust it will be admissible here to call attention to certain remarks frequently made, which have ideas behind them likely many times to work disastrously in their practical application.

It is often said, even by physicians, that a patient "is living on medicine," on stimulants. This is a very common idea both in and out of the profession; and the accepted theory implied in the doctrine of "active medical principles" is responsible for it, — it makes such a belief imperative. As a matter of fact, however, the stimulant is too often hastening the death of the person. We repeat, that the theory of the existence of an agency, — an active principle, not vital, — in association with material medicine, makes the acceptance of such an idea irresistible. That is, the alcoholic spirit agency, or alleged "active medical principle," is presumed temporarily to execute a function which the active *vital* principle cannot execute under the existing circumstances of its enfeebled condition. The text-books allege that "alcoholic spirit gives energy to muscles;" in other words, that it imparts strength. What other inference can be legitimately made on this basis of the accepted doctrine of "active medical principles"?

It is alleged in medical literature that the human mind has no conception of the nature of vital force. This leads us to remark, that the disposition to drink alcoholic spirit, and to use it as a medicine, is based on two misconceptions of serious magnitude. First, the interpretation has been accepted by the profession and the laity that an exchange of sensations effected by alcoholic spirit, — the exchange of a feeling of weariness for a less conscious feeling of weariness, — is satisfactory evidence of a supplied energy. Second, When alcoholic spirit given in a state of collapse has occasioned, as it many times does, a more nearly balanced circulation, the inference has been drawn that this was due to the fact that the "active principle" of the alcohol executed a temporary duty in place of the debilitated vital energy.

When, therefore, it is said that a person is "living on stimulants," it is presumed that the alcoholic "energy," alleged by high medical authority to exist, is running the machinery of life in place of the vital energy. If the accepted doctrine of "active medical properties" were correct, that presumption would be a correct one; and it would also be commendable to urge the people to resort to alcoholic spirit for temporary energy. But should this long-cherished doctrine, like that of the ancient ideal earth-centre, be proven to be an error, a new education will be necessary as a fundamental basis for a successful anti-alcoholic era of prosperity and happiness. I believe that the erroneous idea of the relation of alcoholic spirit to the human organism indoctrinated and perpetuated by the medical profession, is the largest cause of the present evil habit of drinking alcoholic spirit so common among our people. Our citizens of best intelligence and of greatest influence are conscientious in their conviction of the utility of alcoholic spirit for such purposes as advocated by the deluded medical profession; and this conviction prevents the development of that healthy public sentiment which would otherwise exist to protect the people at large from a gross misuse of stimulants.

We ask, now, What is the explanation of recovery from collapse, when such recovery is occasioned by the use of alcoholic stimulation? A person in a condition of collapse — a deficient capillary circulation and cold surface — is given a quantity of alcoholic spirit; and provided that the vital energies are sufficient, the heart's action becomes thereby accelerated, and a larger quantity of blood is sent to the surface instinctively to eliminate the alcohol as a legitimate official function of this vital property. In this way a better balanced circulation is made to prevail which is far more favorable to continued life, even at the expense of more or less vital energy, than was the existing condition of collapse. The vital-power theory, however, would advise that great caution be exercised in such an attempt to balance the circulation with alcoholic spirit relations; while the medical-power theory would permit great liberty in the supply of such expected new energy.

While it would be folly to deny that human life may not in some instances be saved by the use of alcohol as a stimulant, yet if the theory of such use be wrong the tendency will be to continue the practice and destroy the patient. Stimulation as a practice relative to the involuntary life-function is precisely like the application of a whip to the voluntary ability: both will cause a different vital action. Alcoholic stimulation is not a *gift* of energy, but a different *expenditure* of vital energy. Like the use of the whip, it may be available under certain circumstances; but there can be no doubt that it has caused, when given in collapse, ten deaths where it has saved one life. Educa-

tion not only prepares the mind to accept the
inevitable, but also to accept theories based
on imaginary principles; and education
authorizes the giving of alcoholic stimulants
to supply temporary uplifting energy. Indeed, should the physician not resort to such
practice, he is liable to be severely censured
for neglect; and should the patient die from
such treatment, the physician is given much
credit for his perseverance with "active
medical principles." Who ever heard of an
over dose of whiskey for collapse ? Medical
doctrines and theories do not provide for such
a possibility. If the patient lives, it is the
alcoholic energy which saved his life; if
death follows, the patient is charged with a
deficiency of vital ability unequal to swallowing the fluid energy. This is a doctrinal
provision which is very useful in the interests of reconciliation.

In trying to anticipate correctly the future
developments in a human organism diseased
from varied causes, and theorizing from the

old and accepted ideal plan now in use, certain disadvantages will attend the mental operation, such as prevailed with the Ptolemaic theorist when trying to calculate future astronomical events.   The new plan, however, to which we call attention, enables the medical theorist to take advantage in his calculations of all operative principles and laws, as the Copernican system enables the astronomer to do at the present time.

IX.

SENSATION AND SENSIBILITY.

THESE two vital properties have functional relations not previously considered, and which can be described better in a separate chapter, consisting in the fact that each may modify and disturb the function of the other, unlike the relations of previous mention. We can say of those life properties what we have said of the group of zymotic disease, that while they hold a common relation to all things in association with other vital properties, they also have additional relations of inter-association sometimes difficult to illustrate. But all progress in science comes by tedious observation and comparison of Nature's laws and methods; and some things, even if not past finding out, certainly do not become readily apparent.

The vital property sensibility, with some persons, may entertain expectancies of a degree that will develop sensational feelings. For instance, merely the *idea* that an emetic has been administered may produce nausea, and even sensational feelings, to an extent that will cause the function of instinct to exercise involuntary action. Extreme sensational irritability, local or general, may unbalance the function of sensibility to such an extent as to produce delirium and various other disturbances of this vital property. Thus in many cases of mental disturbance, where it is alleged that "the disease has gone to the brain," such condition is produced by sensational irritability, and may frequently be cured by diminishing the cause of such irritability. High temperature of the blood may cause delirium ; also irritability extending over large areas. Nor must we overlook the fact that extreme emotions experienced by the sensibility may so far modify the sensational function as to make favorable or unfavorable the numerous disturbances over which instinct presides. With some persons, in some forms of disease, mental influence constitutes a large factor of the disturbance, and may be made a large factor of the cure. Not only is it possible for each of those vital properties to modify the other, in association with the same individual, but the will-power of one person may modify the function of both sensation and sensibility in another person. This is illustrated in hypnotic influence, which may be carried to such a degree that an amputation can be performed without pain, and even without consciousness.

There are numerous complex operations that are explainable only upon the basis of the co-relation of the several active vital properties. But so long as this department of Nature remains in obscurity, many theories will be adopted to explain such opera-

tions which are untenable in their application. At the same time, such theories may
remain acceptable and yet be as unscientific
in their relation as the alleged and apparent
Indian remedy for eclipse of the moon. Be-
lieving that some animal was about to devour
that satellite, the natives made a great noise
to frighten the animal away; and so far as
appearances were concerned their theory of
a remedy was well supported, and such interpretation was presumed to develop valuable
facts for future guidance in the treatment of
similar inflictions. The Indians were encouraged to believe in the utility of such a
remedy, while at the same time a very
different principle of Nature was implied in
the operation which really produced the
result. The most gigantic modern parallel
of this ancient superstition is illustrated in
the doctrine of "active medical property,"
an imaginary alleged agency, supported by
tons of literature in explanation of its utility,
as a curative and restorative agency; an

active principle and medical agency which is sold to the people with mingled praise and mystery, and which is alleged to act upon and to operate the organs of human life when scientifically harnessed with profound and unspeakable skill.

The modern doctrines of Mind Cure, Mental Healing, and Christian Science are entitled to a candid consideration. There are no working principles in the latter which do not belong to the former, and reversely. Each is in error in its representation of the results claimed from such methods. The doctrine of mental healing has a limited and yet legitimate support in the theory underlying such method, while it has a larger *apparent* support than the nature of the operative principles will warrant. Thus the question arises, to what degree are such results, in other words cures, effected and explainable on the theories advanced in support of such methods ?

Functional diseases of every name and

nature exist either as abnormal sensibilities, — diseases of the mind, — or as abnormal sensations, implied in sensational feelings and involuntary pathological vital actions. We must also recognize that no agency is operative with either the normal or abnormal functions of the living organism, except the vital agency. The mind agency is a vital agency; but the involuntary vital-force agency is not a mind agency. Disease exists in both departments, voluntary and involuntary; and sensation and sensibility have a limited relation of disturbance from each vital property, and also a limited relation in effecting a balance of normal function. Now to what extent are diseases amenable to the mind agency; and what diseases are implied and made operative by that vital force agency which is not a mind agency? This is a larger department of nature than we care to give space for a full explanation of, while it is at the same time entitled to some general outline in association with the subject of this volume.

Notwithstanding that the theories advanced
in support of mental healing are not directly
applicable except with a limited and certain
kind of ailment, the doctrine as a whole
has a better hold on the nature of things, as
a fundamental working principle, than the
alleged agency of an "active medical property." It does have a factor of appropriate
relation as suggested, while the "active
medical property" has none. The mind
agency as a curative agency does apply
directly in some instances, and indirectly in
other instances. Many times the involuntary
vital agency directed by instinct works
out the problem of cure. Whatever theory
may be advanced in explanation of a cure,
the believers and advocates of such theory
will point to their cures and say, "There
is the proof of our theory; there is the living
evidence of the curative influence that has
been operative. You cannot deny facts;
facts are stubborn things." But the "facts"
associated with the Indian's remedy for a

lunar eclipse not only did not refute his theory of remedial measures, but even gave it encouragement ; yet some other theory would explain such facts far more scientifically. It is unquestionably true that some persons do have a wonderful mental influence over certain other persons, but not over all persons to an equal degree. Such influence is directly operative only with a certain class of ailments, largely existing in the voluntary department.

There are two classes of ailments to consider, — those superintended by the mind, and those presided over by instinct. The mind cannot directly guide the activities assigned to the function of instinct. The function of instinct is a reality, it is not imaginary; and to guide this function indirectly it is necessary to make appeal through the vital property sensation. The question then arises, To what extent can the mind produce sensations ? It can to a certain extent, but that extent is very limited. It is a well-known fact that expectancy may induce nausea and vomiting; it may increase or diminish the sensation of pain to a certain degree when due to certain causes, but when due to other causes little or no modification can be effected except with a hypnotic subject.

It is very difficult to comprehend how the mind can abolish those conditions which it cannot produce. The mind cannot produce pneumonia, nor scarlet fever, nor a score of other ailments; and when the mental influence tackles such ailments with an apparent success, please remember the Indian remedy for eclipse. There are different active vital principles implied in such cures wholly unlike mind influence. The mind may exercise a powerful influence for good or for evil in a great variety of ailments. The mind may use up vital energy in worry sufficient to prolong the ailment and even to cause death, in both the voluntary and involuntary departments. It is true also that the mental influence of the patient often constitutes the pivotal influence which may favor a cure or cause death; it is an influence, frequently of pivotal significance, not duly appreciated. Thus it is very important for the attending physician, or "healer," to maintain sufficient control of the hopeful expectancies of his patient to afford the best opportunity for recovery.

It is important, however, to recognize that mind and matter do not constitute the sum total of a human organism. The mind property is but one of four vital properties which exercise functions in the affairs of life. The mind cure, or mental healing, as a theory, like medical theories, is defective; and while frequently fruitful of great practical benefits, all such theories have developed ideal incongruities of nature that may be of profit to review.

It is alleged that pain is not real, only imaginary; that disease exists only in the mind; that both pain and disease are factors

of mind, to be removed at will: thus that
one has only to think strongly that one is
sick or well, and the job is done.   It is true
that in the voluntary department of life
affairs this theory may apply very correctly,
but not in the involuntary.   The mind cannot
will away pneumonia; some other principle
is operative here, and it must have its time.
The doctrine that disease is imaginary, like
the doctrine of "active medical properties,"
has secured a foothold in the popular belief;
and this kind of erroneous interpretation
has grown out of the fact that no recognition
has been developed of the nature of vital
force, or of distinction of functions of the
several ultimate vital properties.

Medical text-books and lexicons fail to
outline the difference between sensation and
sensibility, — those vital properties being
regarded, so far as text-book authority contributes testimony, as each being a part of
the other.   Now, sensation has an innumerable variety of factors; in other words,

11

there are different kinds of sensation, among which are taste, smell, itching, and pain. Sensibility also has a multiplicity of factors that make up the total of that vital property, — emotions of grief, joy, anger, hope, mirth, and reason. Many of the factors of sensibility may be experienced and abolished at will; but pain, being a factor and variety of sensation, cannot be abolished at will. Disease, manifested wholly by the involuntary department, cannot be abolished at will, or cured by mind influence; though such disease may have some of its disagreeable associations modified by mind influence. Involuntary vital power may be guided and controlled to a limited degree by the production of sensations from material contacts, — that being the only means at command which will cause instinct to operate the involuntary vital force as desired.

The human mind requires to be broadened sufficiently to recognize that the human organism is a more complex creation than can be represented through mind and matter; also that it has active vital properties in common with animal life, — so low down in some cases as to have little or no vital property of sensibility; that is, no brain. The complexity of a human organism in its variety of functions is of wonderful extent. Not only are the ultimate vital properties unlike and distinct, but each has factors that make up its whole, of great diversity of function. There are many kinds of tastes and smells and sensational feelings, agreeable and disagreeable; many kinds of sensational happiness, of misery and pain. Sensibility is made up of numerous different factors. Grief is not like joy; sadness is not like hope; and the will power is not like intellectual power. Pain is as real as intelligence, while some people are capable of experiencing more of the former than of the latter. Distress of mind may disturb the functions of other vital properties, while irritability of sensation may unbalance the mind.

In alleged mental healing the result is not all due to mental influence. There are laws of involuntary organic operations — constructive, preservative, and restorative — which to effect, the mind must arrange certain conditions for a successful execution, as would be required for the production of a field of corn. The mental part is frequently more in the arranging than in the *doing*. The medical healers and mental healers have thus far failed to recognize the functions and operative laws through which the vital properties exercise their activities in the affairs of human life, and thus have failed to take ad antage of opportunities that are continually being presented. In consequence thousands of deaths occur annually that might have been prevented. The improper use of medicine is undermining the national health of the people to a degree far more serious than that effected by alcoholic spirit drinking.

In summing up the ideal situation of this

department of Nature as it exists to-day, there are two leading expectancies which we find to predominate. One is the expectancy of great beneficial results from the proper application of an alleged medical agency, — the "active medical property." The other is an expectancy of a mental power that may accomplish a multiplicity of innumerable operations with the organic body, which are really executed by an entirely different agency. Thus the real agency which executes the alleged medical operations, and a very large per cent of the alleged mental cures, — the involuntary vital force, — is not recognized and given credit for its operative function in Nature. And it is also alleged that the nature of this vital force constitutes a problem which must await the advent of future generations for a solution. Therefore, little or nothing of practical importance appears in medical literature relative to this department of involuntary living agency, which would require volumes to elucidate in its application to the various forms of disease.

There are many forms of acute self-limited disease which will be cured in accordance with the laws of involuntary functions committed to the custody of instinct. All kinds of "healers" are likely to take advantage of this fact, and will, unconscious of the principle involved, point to such cures in support of the theory and method they have adopted. Many who claim the discovery of wonderful curative agencies barricade themselves behind the statement, that, while they may not be able to prove that such alleged agency exists, no one can prove that it does not exist. There is much logic in this statement, and it too frequently represents the precise situation. Consequently, no educational authority can expose such frauds with success; and numerous medical and curative systems are invented and become acceptable, while Nature has supplied but one code of laws for disease and the relations thereto of medicine.

X.

WE select this form of disease to illustrate the application of the theory
of Vital Force, not because it is more suit-
able for that purpose, but because it affords a
greater diversity of applied principles.

Starting with the recognition that an
abnormal sensation must precede every form
of disease, the question arises, What constitutes the causes of abnormal sensation in
pneumonia, both primary and secondary?
Among the varied primary causes we mention, first, that frequent cause implied in a
mechanical pressure of blood on the lungs,
together with the accumulation of more or
less effete material which should be eliminated through the skin, — a condition of

unbalanced circulation frequently caused by insufficient clothing for the protection of the body. A great variety of other primary causes may exist, such as inhaled irritant material, — vapors, and extreme cold air; also the presence of poisonous soluble pathological products of previous diseases that are being eliminated through the lungs, constituting primary causes of an abnormal sensation.

Succeeding any one of the primary causes of disease, there is soon a larger quantity of blood in the lung tissues, in association also with an increased temperature of the blood, constituting a secondary cause of great significance, — a congestion and temperature producing an abnormal sensation to a degree of more or less pain. The primary cause, whatever it may be, constitutes but a small factor of causation for the development of pneumonia. Many times the primary cause may exist for a period without disturbing the circulation of the blood sufficient for the production of the secondary cause. It is the nature of instinct to send a larger quantity of blood to any part where an abnormal sensation, or irritability, is made to prevail; thus in a brief time secondary causes are made to exist of serious relations.

Every case of pneumonia would certainly prove fatal, in accordance with the nature and laws of the active ultimate vital properties, were there not provided a principle which we have called "toleration," and which we have explained in a previous chapter. One lung, or a part of one lung, may be thus disturbed without involving all the lung tissues; as is illustrated in superficial inflammation which does not include all adjacent tissues. It is not possible to have pneumonia without an excess of blood in the lung structures; and death ensues because the quantity of blood, together with subsequent pathological changes, mechanically diminishes the air space to a capacity insufficient for respiration. This condition can be made to exist with a strong and vigorous person in forty-eight hours, while with a less vigorous constitution from six to eight days may be required to effect the same condition from congestion and infiltration.

The first change from a normal condition which takes place in the lungs exists as an abnormal sensation, brought about by some of the already mentioned, or similar, primary causes. Instinct sends a larger volume of blood to the lungs in consequence of the irritability which we call abnormal *sensation*. The excess of blood in those organs, and the consequent pathological action, develop continued secondary causes, — high temperature of the blood in most cases being the greater secondary cause which occasions instinct to continue sending an excess of blood to the parts, constituting that condition called inflammation. Thus far, this congestion and inflammation are made to exist in accordance with the nature and laws of the active vital properties; and we repeat

that every case of pneumonia would prove
fatal, did not that self-preservative principle
called "toleration" become effective, which
makes possible that discontinuance of pathological vital action implied in self-limited
disease.

The important feature of treatment in
such cases consists in the early reduction
of the quantity of blood in the lung tissues,
— not by blood-letting, but by diminishing
the secondary cause, heat, which, if allowed
to exist, produces an irritability that will be
a continued cause for instinct to send a
dangerous quantity of blood to those organs.
Diminish the quantity of blood, by reducing the temperature cause of disturbance
of pathological vital action, and thus allow
sufficient air space to be maintained until
toleration is established. There is no occasion to treat primary causes, even were it
possible, but only secondary causes. Exces-
sive temperature is the greatest and most
approachable cause to be treated. The

nerves of the lung tissues easily take on irritability, — a condition that may exist unrecognized by the consciousness, yet having serious relations to instinct. Thus the feelings of the patient are not to be relied upon to determine the severity of existing causes and conditions. The nearer the approach of normal quantity of blood in the lung tissues, the less severe the pneumonia; the nearer that the temperature of the blood is kept to normal, the less cause exists for disturbing the circulation. It is not wise or prudent to try to keep the blood at a normal temperature, but to diminish it several degrees, more or less, from its maximum degree of disturbance.

The practical effect between diminishing the quantity of blood in the lung tissues by blood-letting and lowering of total vital energies by antiphlogistic medication, and that of diminishing the secondary cause, heat, to effect a more nearly balanced circulation, is of great importance to the patient.

This difference is often one of life or death, depending on the method adopted. The best method is to reduce the temperature by conduction, which is always subject to immediate control. Envelop the patient in a wet-sheet pack of varying degrees of temperature, according to the severity of existing abnormal heat. It may be sufficient to envelop the chest with towels wet in cool water, changing every twenty minutes for many hours, sometimes for an entire day, until the temperature is lowered several degrees; and thus keep it reduced for several days from the beginning of the disturbance. The fever thermometer should be used frequently to determine the result of the treatment. A temperature of 104 to 106 degrees demands prompt attention. Do not be afraid of cold water about the chest — but not the extremities — with such temperatures. Do not apply such a degree of cold over large surfaces as to produce a shock of the nervous system. Do not be too heroic in degrees of

cold, but change the appliance more frequently with a milder temperature.

The diminishing of temperature by conduction, in association with opiates, to make
more tolerant the cause of abnormal sensation, constitutes the most reliable treatment
for severe pneumonia as presented by the
sthenic, robust individual. Give the patient
an abundance of cool water, supply the best
air for respiration, and be sparing of food
for the first forty-eight hours.

There are many mild cases of pneumonia
that would recover under almost any let-
alone treatment; and with such cases, much
credit is liable to be given to that method
of treatment which would be of little or no
benefit in severe cases. It is not possible to
cure every case of pneumonia, but fifty per
cent of those robust persons who die without
this treatment would be saved by its early
application. It is the early treatment
which saves, which converts a would-be
severe case into one of milder relations.

The strong, vigorous person is in more danger, because his vital strength can send more blood to the lungs. It would be well for every household to be the possessor of a thermometer, and to know the meaning of a high temperature of the blood, and how safely to reduce it, regardless of what form of disease might be expectant.

With pneumonia, the secondary causes of severe disturbance — *heat* and irritability — must be made less; while with other kinds of disease different secondary causes demand leading attention. In the case of scarlet fever and measles there exists one secondary cause — heat — to be reduced; while that abundant secondary cause of irritability, existing as a poisonous pathological product, must be eliminated. To try to make such cause tolerant would be fatal.

The distinction of the relation of cause between a common cold and pneumonia is but a difference of degree. A "common cold," so called, is caused by a similar disturbance of superficial circulation of the blood, occasioning an abnormal sensation of the mucous membranes. A degree of irritability is thus made to exist only sufficient to cause a local disturbance, with little or no perceptible disturbance of the heart's action; while with pneumonia the degree of irritability is sufficient to disturb the whole system, and occasion the production of a special increased action of the heart, sending an excess of blood to the region of irritation, developing inflammation. The same principle is operative on the external surface, where cause may exist for either irritability or for inflammation.

We repeat, that the causes of disturbance have no influence, do not act, but exist as passive causes, which occasion pathological vital action to develop. Medicine has no "active medical property;" it is passive, and a cause for a different vital act. There is no medical agency that can do duty in substitution for vital force; but medicine may

be made useful to modify conditions, and
to cause sensation to be more tolerant.   It
may be used to produce a sensation which
will occasion the deployment of vital activity
for the execution of such act as may seem
wise to have established.

The theory of the Science of Vital Force
fits every form of disease equally as well as
it does pneumonia; and each form as well
as severity of unlike disease has special
features entitled to consideration, which
could not be illustrated except in association
with a description of such disease.   Vital
force acts in relation to nutrient material with
normal surroundings, and produces health.
Vital force acts in relation to non-nutrient
material and abnormal surroundings, and
produces disease.

The relation of medicine to the human
organism is represented in two distinct
divisions.   In one division its relation consists in the production of a sensation from
contact, without disturbance and develop-

ment of pathological vital action. There are different kinds of sensations innumerable. The other division is implied in the production of sensations that are succeeded by pathological vital actions directed by instinct. This action is usually called "the action of the medicine." The different kinds of pathological action are also innumerable.

Thus, in brief, we legitimately use medicine either to produce and modify sensations, or to develop pathological vital actions. Certain causes of disease produce abnormal sensations more or less disagreeable, without development of pathological actions, which constitute one form of disease. Certain other causes also produce abnormal sensations that *are* succeeded by pathological vital actions directed by instinct, which actions *do* constitute active disease. Functional disease is pathological vital action; and the active effects from medicinal relations constitute a similar representation of an involuntary active vital principle.

In the disease called "pneumonia" there is no occasion to give medicines to deploy and develop pathological actions, but only to modify sensations for the purpose of diminishing pathological vital actions.

MISCELLANEOUS PARAGRAPHS.

Science. The uplifting of astronomical science from its crude associations was effected by a recognition of the true centre of the solar system; and with the department of medical science there are accepted theories and fallacious ideas to be eliminated, as well as a recognition to be obtained of a different plan, implied in the four ultimate active vital properties of human life functions and their co-operative relations.

Little or no progress can be made in establishing fundamental principles on which a scientific practice of medicine may be predicated, essential both to intellectual pride and a more successful result, until all beliefs and ideas are eliminated of an existing agency in Nature called "active medical property," implied in an active principle alleged to be stored away in roots, barks, and minerals, which is said to act on the organs of human life. This accepted idea, now taught and perpetuated, is as crude and void of all representation of a fact or principle in Nature as the doctrine of a flat earth and the ancient ideal centre of the solar system.

In calling attention to the Science of Vital Force, and to the necessary revolution of ideas following upon it, there is presented a subject never paralleled in importance in all the events of civilization and the development of a science. In association with such a revolution in the department of astronomical science, history is responsible for the statement that the human mind had so little ability to exercise rational thought that it required more than a century to eliminate the crude ideas of the old traditional system, even after public attention was

called to its monstrous delusions. So also
it may not be unreasonable to expect that
some minds will prove to be so fixed by
previous education, so inflexible and inca-
pable of progress, that it will not be possible
for them to unlearn the ideal fallacies of
medical teaching that have stamped their
impress upon the public mind by the aid of
those authorities whose business it is supposed to be to transmit wisdom.   But in the
recognition and development of the Science
of Vital Force, Nature must be accepted as
the highest authority.

Organic disease.   In previous pages, frequent mention has been made of abnormal
sensation and pathological vital actions;
and with organic disease, the phrase abnormal construction is appropriate in representation of the displacement of normal cell
structure by a malignant cell growth.

Functional disease is pathological vital
action, and pathological vital action in the
affairs of cell structure may develop malig-

nant growth. Thus there may exist pathological vital action which is not implied in cell construction, while at other times such perversion of activity may become manifest only in abnormal cell construction. When seeking to comprehend the cause of such formation, it is necessary to invoke the aid of the several functions of vital properties.

In the formation of normal cell structure there is implied a surrounding condition of normal sensation; while in the construction of malignant growth there evidently prevails a condition of abnormal sensation, — a condition of local irritation of a period of shorter or longer duration. Thus in looking for a cause, we cannot go behind the relative difference between normal and abnormal sensation, — the local irritation alone being the modifying influence causing the construction of malignant cells in place of normal cell structure. *Why* a local irritation, which is of frequent existence, may sometimes be followed by such change of cell structure

and not at other times is a problem difficult
to solve. It is difficult to explain fully why
a certain cause of disease at one time may
not produce disease every time and with
every person, — although such explanation,
if possible, would not be implied in the
nature and relation of the cause, but in
some existing condition of the individual.

The theory we present of active vital force
based on the functions of the several vital
properties, as well as the facts of common
recognition, contributes support and evidence to the fact that malignant growth may
succeed to known conditions of local irritability, — as may be illustrated in cancer of
the mouth from irritable gums, produced by
incrustations and decayed teeth. It is
alleged by high authority that a mechanical
injury from a blow has been succeeded by
malignant growth. Sometimes in organic
disease of the liver and kidneys succeeding
long-continued existing local disturbance,
occasioned by the presence of alcoholic spirit

in near proximity to cell structure, there is illustrated the same principle and relation of cause. Thus we might say that the normal cell growth is handicapped by the presence of such material, and that in place of normal sensation there exists a local irritation, constituting the modified surroundings which favor, in place of normal cell growth, that modification of cell structure implied in organic disease. The cause of disease does not act; it only causes an abnormal sensation, which perverts vital action.

In the studious research to connect the "germ theory of disease" with cancerous growth, there has been discovered in some instances a protozoic parasite; and a distinguished writer thus states: "It seems difficult to grasp how the chronic irritation or the toxic influence of a parasite can produce, for instance, a cancer." There is no "toxic influence," but only a toxic *relation*. The "toxic influence" is an ideal outgrowth from the erroneous doctrine implied in the accepted theory that causes *act*. The material of toxic contact relation disturbs the instinctive influence; abnormal sensation is produced, and instinct constructs a pathological cell growth, — malignant structure. So far as the parasite is concerned, we assume that this alleged "germ" took up its abode in that region after irritability was established, and perhaps after malignant cells began to form. Even be it otherwise, the relation of such parasite could be of no different kind than as a cause of abnormal sensation. Sensation, normal or abnormal, is the first language of life, from the contact relation of the external world to a living human organism.

Alcoholic stimulation. Alcoholic spirit consumption, both as a beverage and for medicinal use, is a custom encouraged by a certain kind of scientific education, and confirmed by the temporary experience of "*feeling* better." All the pleasures of life are experienced through the vital properties sensation and sensibility; and the fact that alcoholic spirit may occasion a more agreeable sensation, in substitute for such disagreeable sensations as weariness and hunger, — thus effecting a swapping of sensations, which has been given the interpretation of a contribution of energy, — constitutes the great educational influence for the adoption of this practice. There also exists the testimony of high medical authority, as well as the influence of the object lessons of practice, that alcoholic stimulation is implied in the alleged action of the "active medical property" of the alcoholic spirit, acting as a temporary substitute for vital energy. If such stimulation were really a temporary supply of energy, as alleged by medical authority, alcoholic spirit would be a very useful article of consumption; but such is not the fact. If the swapping of sensations were truly scientific evidence of supplied strength, alcoholic spirit would be a household remedy of great utility; but such is not the fact.

Neither the swapping of sensations nor stimulation constitutes a contribution of energy.
Stimulation is not the exercise of an "active
medical principle," but an expenditure of
vital energy,— a differently deployed vital
action, holding the same relation to the
involuntary vital action that the whip holds
to the voluntary.

The alcoholic spirit question is a larger
subject with which to contend than has been
recognized by the most zealous workers in
the field of reform.   The alcoholic infliction
of misery is not a sequence of human depravity, but of a false scientific culture.
The worst foe of the temperance cause unconsciously exists in the acceptance of erroneous medical doctrines, and in the inability
to distinguish an occasioned agreeable sensation from a contribution of strength.   Should
the workers in the temperance cause expend
a part of their energies and money in the
development of a new education, it would
contribute a hundred fold more to the success

of the reform than the effort of applied legislative coercion to overcome an unconscious
educational influence.   Public sentiment is
wrong.   Public sentiment, however, is not
a spontaneous outgrowth, but dependent on
education; it is what the people make it on
an educational basis.   It is an all-powerful
influence for the right or the wrong, as the
case may be.   The evils of alcoholic spirit
drinking cause its practice to be condemned,
while the culture for the persuasion of such
practice is allowed to be perpetuated, —
which balances the opposing influence, as
the statistics of consumption demonstrate.
The practice is allowed, because it is sus-
tained by medical authority, — an authority
not prudent to deny, without a reserve corps
of natural fundamental principles at command for support.   If the temperance workers
are in earnest, they should make it known
that science is the natural ally of temperance, and not the persuader of the use of
alcoholic spirit as a vehicle of "active medical property."

The medical profession. Who shall prac-
tise medicine ?   Who shall treat the sick and
superintend the management of disease ?

This is a difficult question to adjust on the
basis of ability and satisfaction to all par-
ties; and it is a very much discussed question at the present time.   We must recognize that all people have *rights*, while a
lesser number have *abilities*.   It would seem,
however, that this question must ultimately
be settled on the same basis as is implied in
the question of who should be allowed to
make astronomical calculations, and who
should be allowed to make a chemical analy-
sis of the contents of a human stomach.   So
long as medical science remains acceptable
in its present crude state of imaginary fundamental principles, there is no authority that
can demonstrate where to draw the line and
determine on which side exists capability,
and on which side exists uncapability, to pre-
scribe for and to manage disease.   So long
as the real fundamental principles of this

department are allowed to remain in obscurity, and success is hoped for through the agency of some wonderful medical power, which is as liable to be discovered by an ignoramus and mere speculator as by a cultured physician, this will be a difficult question to settle. So long as "active medical properties" rather than active mental abilities are recognized and presumed to be of the greatest utility, this subject will continue to be agitated. So long as the people believe that a medicine can *act* and exercise activity with the organs of life, and remain uneducated relative to the nature and functions of the unlike ultimate vital agencies and the required guidance of such agency in the affairs of disease, the judgment of such ability will be subject to the whims of ignorance. An ignoramus and speculator in human misfortunes, when giving *placeboes* for a self-limited disease which is sure to get well if let alone, is liable to be credited with as much skill, erudition, and ability as the cultured physician.

The fundamental premises of this subject exist as a blank in the minds of the people, which allows them to be unconsciously imposed upon to a degree of criminality and the sacrifice of life. There are no recognized fundamental principles of educational acquirement that are accepted as a superior qualification for professional practice. Every school of medicine and treatment has a set of alleged fundamental principles of conventional adoption, while Nature has provided but one code of laws and principles that are operative in the affairs of disease. As there is but one science of astronomy and one science of chemistry, so there is but one science of medicine. When the people are educated to understand the nature of the premises on which a scientific treatment and practice of medicine is based, it would be a very ignorant invalid, surrounded by ignorant advisers, who would permit an alleged physician to attempt the guidance of his involuntary vital force in conditions of disease who was not well educated in the science of this department of Nature. There are provided principles and operative laws for a more successful treatment and practice of medicine not yet recognized and taught for the benefit of a civilized people; and when this department is understood, the medical profession will occupy a much higher position both in reality and in the judgment of the people, — a position of greater utility to individual and national prosperity than has ever been achieved through any department of scholastic attainment.

Conclusion. We are aware that the theory of the Science of Vital Force has been presented in these pages with much assurance; but it is an assurance born of the conviction that these operative fundamental principles will stand the test of severe criticism, being based on the living laws of this department of Nature, and capable of demonstration in verified phenomena presented in the human organism.

13

The practical utility of this science transcends all other departments of accumulated wisdom in its applicability to the preservation of human life and recovery from disease, enabling us to adopt measures for the saving of human life at present unrecognized. It affords protection against the infatuation of the alcoholic delusion of expectancy, and merits the attention of earnest workers in temperance reform as the most powerful ally for the development of a higher public sentiment, based on scientific achievements. It illustrates that ignorance, not depravity, is responsible for the alcoholic infliction which has come upon a civilized people. It enables demonstrated science to become an ally of temperance reform, while at the present time alleged science is the worst unconscious enemy of the temperance movement.

Statesmen allege that the temperance question is the greatest national question before the people of this generation; but we affirm that the Science of Vital Force is much the larger subject, for it includes and furnishes a solution for the former, which is implied in that enigmatical paradox where two unlike educations on the subject prevail at the same time, — one persuading to the use of alcoholic spirit for the benefit of its expectant active principle of temporary energy, while the other persuades to its abolishment on the records of its practical effects. When the utility and advantages of this science become recognized, it will be important to have elementary text-books prepared for use in common schools, from which a general outline of the subject may be taught in association with the temperance education so much needed, — a subject no more profound than the general principles on which the science of astronomy is based, and certainly of greater practical benefit. There should also be prepared a temperance edition for the development of a higher educational standard of public sentiment, including a household department of instruction, contributing in-

formation for the preservation of health and
the management of disease pending the arri-
val of a physician, who would be required to
be familiar with this department of science
before his services would become acceptable
to a cultured people.

The time is coming in the near future
when it will be considered necessary for the
public good that each State supply, or provide at cost, such a book of instruction for
every family; for the prosperity of our coun-
try is dependent on educational development.
There exists an opportunity unprecedented
in this direction for the labors of some phi-
lanthropic association to develop such commendable innovation in the interests of
humanity and a better civilization. When
the ideal centre of the solar system was
changed, astronomical literature required
to be rewritten; and it is of much greater
importance in this department relating to
temperance, the preservation of health, and
recovery from disease.   Physicians' text-

books on theory and practice will require to be rewritten, illustrating the advantages of the applied science of vital force in guiding the treatment of disease; and the day is not far distant when every medical school will have an instructor in this department.

The nature of this subject forbids all rivalry of claim for superiority of advantage in any particular pathy. There is but one science of disease and relation of medicine. Every practitioner, prescriber, superintendent, and general manager of diseased conditions should have an education sufficiently broad to take in the whole system. The emergency of the situation requires that the nature, management, and treatment of disease shall be presented in a new form and upon a different basis, — the basis of demonstrated fundamental principles implied in the science of vital force. No branch of scientific education exists to-day in such a deplorable and dangerous situation for practical appliance as the department of alleged medical science.

The accepted doctrine of "active medical properties" is as fallacious as the ancient ideal centre of the solar system, while, practically, the application of this imaginary *active principle* is destroying many thousands of human lives annually. There is not an intelligent person among civilized nations who will compare the phenomena presented by the human organism with the alleged science of vital force without adopting a similar conclusion. And the intelligent people of this generation who are liable to become victims of this dangerous delusion, cannot afford to extend the mistaken courtesy of silence relative to this alleged department of nature, but should immediately demand for individual and national protection a higher standard of medical culture.

THE END.